NEW VANGUARD 198

IMPERIAL JAPANESE NAVY DESTROYERS 1919–45 (1)

Minekaze to Shiratsuyu Classes

MARK STILLE ILLUSTRATED BY PAUL WRIGHT

First published in Great Britain in 2013 by Osprey Publishing,
Midland House, West Way, Botley, Oxford, OX2 0PH, UK
43-01 21st Street, Suite 220B, Long Island City, NY 11101, USA
E-mail: info@ospreypublishing.com

Osprey Publishing is part of the Osprey Group

© 2013 Osprey Publishing Ltd.

All rights reserved. Apart from any fair dealing for the purpose of private study, research, criticism or review, as permitted under the Copyright, Designs and Patents Act, 1988, no part of this publication may be reproduced, stored in a retrieval system, or transmitted in any form or by any means, electronic, electrical, chemical, mechanical, optical, photocopying, recording or otherwise, without the prior written permission of the copyright owner. Inquiries should be addressed to the Publishers.

A CIP catalog record for this book is available from the British Library

Print ISBN: 978 1 84908 984 5
PDF e-book ISBN: 978 1 84908 986 9
EPUB e-book ISBN: 978 1 84908 985 2

Index by Sandra Shotter
Typeset in Sabon and Myriad Pro
Originated by PDQ Media, Bungay, UK
Printed in China through Worldprint Ltd.

13 14 15 16 17   10 9 8 7 6 5 4 3 2 1

www.ospreypublishing.com

Osprey Publishing is supporting the Woodland Trust, the UK's leading woodland conservation charity, by funding the dedication of trees.

ACKNOWLEDGEMENTS

The author would like to thank the Yamato Museum, Tohru Kizu, editor of *Ships of the World Magazine* and Robert Hanshew at the Naval History and Heritage Command Photographic Section for their help in procuring the photographs for this book. Allyn Nevitt also provided a valuable review of the text and his work on the Combined Fleet website is an outstanding resource for deeper research into the histories of the Imperial Navy's destroyers. Thanks also go to Tony Holmes for his assistance in translating key passages of source material.

CONTENTS

INTRODUCTION   4

JAPANESE NAVAL STRATEGY AND THE ROLE OF THE DESTROYER   4

JAPANESE DESTROYER DESIGN PRINCIPLES   5

JAPANESE DESTROYER WEAPONS   6
- Torpedoes
- Guns
- Anti-aircraft Armament
- Japanese Destroyer Radar

MINEKAZE CLASS   8
- Design and Construction
- Armament and Service Modifications
- Wartime Service

KAMIKAZE CLASS   12
- Design and Construction
- Armament and Service Modifications
- Wartime Service

MUTSUKI CLASS   16
- Design and Construction
- Armament and Service Modifications
- Wartime Service

FUBUKI CLASS   21
- Design and Construction
- Armament and Service Modifications
- Wartime Service

AKATSUKI CLASS   30
- Design and Construction
- Armament and Service Modifications
- Wartime Service

HATSUHARU CLASS   35
- Design and Construction
- Armament and Service Modifications
- Wartime Service

SHIRATSUYU CLASS   39
- Design and Construction
- Armament and Service Modifications
- Wartime Service

ANALYSIS AND CONCLUSION   46

BIBLIOGRAPHY   47

INDEX   48

IMPERIAL JAPANESE NAVY DESTROYERS 1919–45 (1)
MINEKAZE TO SHIRATSUYU CLASSES

INTRODUCTION

During the Pacific War of 1941–45, arguably the most successful component of the Imperial Japanese Fleet was its destroyer force. These ships were generally larger than their Allied counterparts and were better armed in most cases. Equipped with a large, long-range torpedo (eventually called "Long Lance" by the Allies), these ships proved themselves as formidable opponents. In the first part of the war, Japanese destroyers were instrumental in an unbroken string of Japanese victories. However, it was not until the Guadalcanal campaign of 1942–43 that these ships fully demonstrated their power. In a series of night actions, these ships devastated Allied task forces in a number of attacks using their deadly torpedoes.

This volume will detail the history, weapons, and tactics of the Japanese destroyers built before World War II. This includes the famous Fubuki class (called "Special Type" by the Japanese), which was the most powerful class of destroyer in the world when completed in the late 1920s. This design forced all other major navies to follow suit and provided the basic design for the many later classes of Imperial Navy destroyers. The first seven classes of the Imperial Navy's fleet destroyers that saw service between 1941 and 1945 (74 ships) are included in this volume. Another book will cover the remainder of the classes, including the Matsu class of destroyer escorts.

JAPANESE NAVAL STRATEGY AND THE ROLE OF THE DESTROYER

The First Destroyer Squadron at anchor sometime in the 1930s. A Sendai-class light cruiser is the flagship, with nine *Kamikaze* and *Minekaze* destroyers anchored behind. The destroyer squadron was the basis for massed night torpedo attacks. (Naval History and Heritage Command)

During the interwar years, the Imperial Navy put considerable thought into the nature of the expected clash with the US Navy. Because the Washington Naval Treaty of 1922 locked them into a position of inferiority with regard to capital ships, the Japanese were fixated on the problem of how they could overcome the larger American Navy during a single decisive engagement. The solution devised by the Japanese was an attrition strategy to reduce the American advantage in capital ships before the climactic engagement. The principal part of this strategy

Several Mutsuki-class destroyers in a pre-war review. At the start of the war, the Mutsuki class comprised three destroyer divisions. Massed destroyer attack was an integral part of Japanese naval doctrine. (*Ships of the World*)

was sustained night attacks by torpedo-equipped units before the final battleships' duel. Within this framework, destroyers were expected to play a key role.

Before the war, Japanese destroyers were organized into divisions of three or four ships, each almost always equipped with ships of the same class. Three or four divisions composed a squadron, which was led by a light cruiser that had command spaces big enough to act as a flagship. Destroyer squadrons were expected to attack en masse during night combat to deliver shattering blows to the enemy. In the 1934 battle instructions, each destroyer squadron was supported by a division of heavy cruisers, which provided combat power to permit the destroyers to penetrate the enemy's screen to attack his battle line. If all went according to the carefully choreographed and rehearsed sequence, the heavy cruisers would open the night battle with a massed torpedo assault, followed by a massed attack by the destroyer squadrons at close range. The destroyers would fire their first torpedo load, then disengage, reload, and fire a second barrage. This decisive battle never took place during the war, but the tactics practiced by the Japanese destroyers proved devastating on a number of occasions.

JAPANESE DESTROYER DESIGN PRINCIPLES

The growing Imperial Navy took an early interest in torpedo boats. As early as 1879, the Japanese began ordering torpedo boats from British, French, and German yards. Increasingly, many of these boats were built in Japan using foreign parts and foreign designs. By 1898, construction of larger British destroyer designs was begun. These boats played important roles in the war against Imperial Russia in 1904–05 and reinforced the Japanese belief that torpedo boats were an important component of the fleet. Coming out of the war with Russia, the Japanese concentrated on building destroyers of British design in Japan.

By the onset of World War I, the Japanese were short of modern destroyers. In response, construction began on a class of ships based on a British design, but fitted with a heavier armament than comparable British and German ships. By the end of the war, Japanese destroyer construction had diverged into two paths, a first-class destroyer of around 1,300 tons with three or four 4.7in. guns and six 21in. torpedo tubes, and a second-class destroyer of some 850 tons with three 4.7in. guns and six torpedo tubes.

Throughout this design evolution, the Japanese placed emphasis on the destroyer as a platform to bring a heavy torpedo load against the enemy battle line. This meant the Japanese favored larger ships with a heavy torpedo armament. This translated into a ship maximized for surface engagements at the expense of other missions. This approach was epitomized by the introduction of the "Special Type" destroyers, which carried an impressive torpedo armament. This basic design precept was carried forward to the next five classes of Japanese destroyers. This also marked the Japanese destroyer as primarily an offensive weapon, maximized for its role as a night-combat torpedo platform.

JAPANESE DESTROYER WEAPONS

Torpedoes

The key weapon aboard Japanese destroyers was the torpedo. The Minekaze and Kamikaze classes carried six torpedoes in three Type 6 twin launchers. These ships used the 6th Year Type 21in. torpedo developed in 1917. The Mutsuki class introduced the 24in. torpedo and the Type 12 triple launcher. The Special Type destroyer also used the Type 12 launcher. The Mutsuki and Special Type ships used the 8th Year Type torpedo developed in 1919, and then the Type 90, which was introduced in 1930. This was the weapon in use at the start of the war. By the end of 1942, the use of the Type 90 was discontinued.

The signature Japanese destroyer weapon of the Pacific War was the Type 93 torpedo. This was a revolutionary weapon, which used oxygen as the torpedo propellant. This was a much more powerful source of energy that enabled much greater ranges. The use of compressed oxygen also created space for a much larger warhead and offered nearly wakeless running. After a long development period, the torpedo entered service in 1935. The range and power of this weapon was far in excess of the standard American destroyer torpedo, and thus its potential was not understood by the Americans until 1943. Eventually it was named "Long Lance" by the Americans, after it had sunk or crippled numerous American and Allied ships. The Hatsuharu class used the Type 90 triple launcher to employ the Type 93 and subsequent classes used the Type 92 quad launcher.

A Group I Special Type destroyer with its three triple-torpedo mounts trained to port. The torpedo broadside of the Special Type destroyers made them formidable offensive platforms. (*Ships of the World*)

Japanese Destroyer-launched Torpedoes				
	6th Year Type	8th Year Type	Type 90	Type 93
Length	22ft 5in.	27ft 7in.	27ft 10in.	29ft 6in.
Diameter	21in.	24in.	24in.	24in.
Weight	3,157lb	5,207lb	5,734lb	5,940lb
Warhead	441lb	761lb	825lb	1,078lb
Propulsion	Steam	Steam	Steam	Oxygen
Speed/Range	36kt / 7,650yd	38kt / 10,900yd	46kt / 7,650yd	48kt / 21,900yd
	32kt / 10,900yd	32kt / 16,400yd	43kt / 10,900yd	40kt / 35,000yd
	26kt / 16,400yd	28kt / 21,900yd	35kt / 16,400yd	36kt / 43,700yd

This is a close-up view of the aft 4.7in. gun on destroyer *Mikatsuki* after she was beached and destroyed in July 1943. The breechblock of the gun has been removed, but this view shows the later type of shield mounted on Mutsuki-class units. (Naval History and Heritage Command)

Guns

Older Japanese destroyers carried four hand-worked single 4.7in. guns. These were exposed mounts provided with only a small shield. Beginning with the Special Type units, the size of the main battery was increased to a 5in. gun. For the first time ever on any destroyer, the gun was provided with an enclosed shield. This was only 3mm thick, but it provided protection from the weather. The first ten Special Type units were fitted with the Type A twin mount, with a maximum 40-degree elevation. The later Special Type ships introduced the Type B mount, which had a 75-degree elevation in an attempt to make the mounts capable of anti-aircraft fire. However, training and elevation were so slow that these mounts were useless in this role. The Shiratsuyu class introduced the Type C mount with a 55-degree elevation. The failure of the Japanese to develop a true dual-purpose 5in. gun for destroyer use became a critical weakness later in the war as Japanese destroyers were increasingly exposed to American air attack. The twin mount also had a dispersion problem when employed against surface targets.

Japanese Destroyer Main Guns		
	4.7in./45 3rd Year (1914)	5in./50 3rd Year
Shell weight	45lb	50.7lb
Muzzle velocity	2,707ft/sec	2,986–3,002ft/sec
Firing cycle	12sec	6–12sec
Maximum range	17,500yd	20,100yd

Anti-aircraft Armament

Going into the war, Japanese destroyers possessed totally inadequate anti-aircraft protection. Only light weapons were in use, and the only intermediate size weapon, the Vickers 40mm single mount introduced in 1927, proved a failure in service. Older ships carried single 7.7mm Lewis guns at the start of the war. Special Type units carried a paltry one or two twin 13mm mounts, which were license-built from a French design. Later in the war, single 13mm mounts were introduced to increase the number of guns available for anti-aircraft protection.

The standard Japanese anti-aircraft gun of the war was the Type 96 25mm weapon introduced in 1936 and first fitted aboard the Asashio class in 1937. Later, triple- and single-mount versions were introduced. It was an unfortunate choice as the standard destroyer anti-aircraft weapon because it had many shortcomings, including low training and elevating speeds, excessive muzzle blast, and a rate of fire that was reduced by the need to keep reloading 15-round magazines. Later in the war, the twin mount was replaced by a triple mount and, in a desperate bid to further increase the numbers of anti-aircraft weapons in 1944, single mounts were placed on destroyers wherever a clear arc of fire was possible. Despite the growing profusion of 25mm guns, Japanese destroyers grew increasingly vulnerable to air attack throughout the war.

Type 96 25mm Gun (1936)	
Muzzle velocity	984yd/sec
Rate of fire	220–40rpm theoretical; 110–20rpm actual
Anti-aircraft range	Maximum 8,200yd; effective range 766–1,633yd
Shell weight	8.8oz

Japanese Destroyer Radar

Japanese destroyers did not begin the war equipped with radar. Not until mid-1943 did select destroyers finally receive the No. 22 radar. This was a twin-horn set, one for transmitting and one for receiving, designed for surface search. Destroyer foremasts were modified to allow the placement of the No. 22 radar above the bridge structure, and a radar room was built further down the foremast. Specifications for the radar are provided below, but unlike American radars the No. 22 was not accurate enough to provide for control of gunnery. Early Japanese radars were unreliable and their operators often poorly trained. Even after the introduction of radar, and certainly in the first part of the war, the first indication that a Japanese destroyer captain received of an approaching enemy, even at night, was from one of his lookouts using high-quality optics. Reliance on optics instead of electronics became increasingly problematic as the Americans introduced better radars and became increasingly adept at their use. During the night battles off the Solomon Islands between August and November 1943, the lack of modern radar was the single most important factor, leading to heavy losses by the Japanese destroyer force.

In 1944 most surviving destroyers received radar designed for air search in an attempt to provide a greater measure of protection from air attack. This was the No. 13 radar, which had a long ladder antenna and was usually fitted on the mainmast of destroyers.

Japanese Destroyer Radars

	No. 13	No.22 Mod. 4M
Peak power output	10kW	2kW
Maximum range	93 miles	37 miles
Effective range		
(single aircraft)	31 miles	11 miles
(group of aircraft)	62 miles	22 miles
Accuracy	2,187–3,280yd	273–546yd
Bearing accuracy	10 degrees	3 degrees

For surface targets, the No.22 (4) could detect a battleship target at 38,276yd, a cruiser-sized ship at 21,872yd, and a destroyer-sized target at 18,591yd. The range error was 820–1,640ft and the bearing error up to 3 degrees.

MINEKAZE CLASS

Design and Construction

Following World War I, the Japanese began development of a new first-class destroyer design. Fifteen of these ships were ordered in the 1917–20 programs and units began to enter the fleet in 1920. These ships were originally only given numbers, as were all destroyers up through the Special Type, until 1928, when they were assigned names.

Minekaze Class Construction

Ship	Built at	Laid down	Launched	Completed
Akikaze	Nagasaki by Mitsubishi	06/07/20	12/14/20	04/01/21
Hakaze	Nagasaki by Mitsubishi	11/11/18	06/21/20	09/16/20
Hokaze	Maizuru Navy Yard	11/30/20	07/12/21	12/22/21
Minekaze	Maizuru Navy Yard	04/20/18	02/08/19	03/29/20
Namikaze	Maizuru Navy Yard	11/07/21	06/24/22	11/11/22
Nokaze	Maizuru Navy Yard	04/16/21	10/01/21	03/31/22
Numakaze	Maizuru Navy Yard	08/10/21	02/25/22	07/24/22
Okikaze	Maizuru Navy Yard	02/22/19	10/03/19	08/17/20
Sawakaze	Nagasaki by Mitsubishi	01/07/18	01/07/19	03/16/20
Shiokaze	Maizuru Navy Yard	05/15/20	10/22/20	07/29/21
Tachikaze	Maizuru Navy Yard	08/18/20	03/31/21	12/05/21
Yakaze	Nagasaki by Mitsubishi	08/15/18	04/10/20	07/19/20
Yukaze	Nagasaki by Mitsubishi	12/24/20	05/28/21	08/24/21

The new class was a hybrid of traditional British and German destroyer designs, as the Imperial Navy had been exposed to German design techniques after receiving

Minekaze shown in August 1932. This view shows the raised forecastle and the well in front of the bridge structure. The four 4.7in. guns are also visible, as is the forward torpedo mount under canvas. This configuration was maintained up until the start of the Pacific War. (Yamato Museum)

five German destroyers after the war as reparations. Design requirements for the new class called for a larger ship with a higher speed. Another important design consideration was seaworthiness, which was an important factor since the waters of the Western and Northern Pacific could be very rough. To meet the requirements for seaworthiness, Japanese designers employed a design component from German destroyers by moving the bridge back and placing a well in front of the bridge. This well area was meant to reduce the impact of heavy seas on the bridge. The forecastle was lengthened and a turtleback aspect given to the forward part of the ship.

To increase the utility of the main guns in heavy seas, the main battery was positioned as high up on the ship as possible, and all guns were sited on the centerline. The last three ships of the class (*Nokaze*, *Namikaze* and *Numakaze*) were built to a slightly different design and are often referred to as the Nokaze class. Instead of placing two 4.7in. guns amidships, the arrangement was modified so that only one gun remained between the stacks and two were mounted together on the aft deckhouse. This allowed for better ammunition-handling arrangements.

To meet the requirement for high speeds, the ships were fitted with geared turbines, replacing the direct drive turbines on earlier destroyer classes. These were capable of 38,500 shaft horse power (SHP), which translated to a maximum speed of 39kt.

This basic design was used for the next three classes of Japanese destroyers, a total of 36 ships. Until the advent of the Special Type destroyers in 1929, these 36 ships constituted the core of the Japanese destroyer force.

Armament and Service Modifications

Minekaze-class units were launched with an armament of three twin 21in. torpedo mounts. One mount was positioned in the well in front of the bridge structure and the other two abaft the second stack. The main gun battery was comprised of four 4.7in. single guns. These were positioned one forward and one aft, with the other two amidships. These were open mounts exposed to the weather except for a small shield. Two 6.5mm machine guns were also fitted upon completion.

This 1928 view of *Nokaze* shows the appearance of the last three units of the Minekaze class. The aft two 4.7in. guns have been located together on the aft superstructure. (Yamato Museum)

This fine beam view of *Okikaze* from November 1932 shows the placement of the main battery and the three torpedo mounts, all under canvas. The ship's name is presented on the side of the hull. The number "2" on the bow is the ship's parent destroyer division. (Yamato Museum)

As war approached, the Minekaze class ships were considered second-line units. Before the war, *Nadakaze* and *Shimakaze* were converted into destroyer transports and renumbered Patrol Boats 1 and 2. In 1941, *Sawakaze* had most of her armament removed for conversion into an aircraft rescue ship. The remaining 12 units in the class received modifications in keeping with their new role as escorts. The two amidships 4.7in. guns were removed, as were the two aft torpedo mounts. The anti-aircraft armament was increased to as many as ten 25mm guns. The minesweeping gear on the fantail was removed and replaced by four depth-charge launchers and 36 depth charges. The increased displacement reduced speed to 35kt.

By September 1942, *Yakaze* was largely disarmed and converted into a target ship. In 1944, the surviving ships were further modified to augment their anti-aircraft fit. The number of 25mm guns was increased to between 13 and 20, with a combination of twin and single mounts. Most ships also received 13mm machine guns.

Two ships surviving into 1945 underwent conversion into *kaiten* (manned torpedo) carriers. *Namikaze* and *Shiokaze* had their sterns modified so that *kaiten*s could be launched astern. *Shiokaze* could carry as many as four *kaiten*s; *Namikaze* only two. Both had all their torpedo tubes removed and retained only their forward 4.7in. gun. Anti-aircraft armament was six twin 25mm mounts and a number of single 25mm mounts. *Namikaze* was fitted with a No. 22 radar on her foremast, while *Shiokaze* received a No. 13 radar on her mainmast. Other ships to receive radar included *Yukaze*, which received a No. 13 set, and *Sawakaze*, which was fitted with a No. 22 radar. *Sawakaze* was fitted with an experimental 5.9in. anti-submarine rocket launcher in place of the forward 4.7in. gun. Her speed was reduced to 16kt.

Wartime Service

Akikaze: She began the war assigned to Destroyer Division 34, subordinate to the Eleventh Air Fleet, and supported the invasion of the Philippines and later the Dutch East Indies and Malaya during the initial period of the war. By June 1942, she had moved to Rabaul, where she supported operations in the Solomons and New Guinea. In August, she suffered heavy damage in an air attack south of Rabaul. She was again damaged by air attack in December 1943, but repaired at Truk. In 1944, she was assigned to duties in the Central Pacific. She participated in the Battle of Leyte Gulf in October 1944, and was sunk off Luzon on November 3, 1944 by the American submarine *Pintado*.

Hakaze: She began the war assigned to Destroyer Division 34. During the first months of the war, she was active in the South China Sea area moving airbase materials from Indochina to Borneo and Malaya. In April 1942, she moved to Rabaul to support the upcoming invasion of Port Moresby. She conducted several transport runs to Munda on New Georgia Island in support of airfield construction there. On January 23, 1943, she was torpedoed off Kavieng by the American submarine *Guardfish*.

Hokaze: At the start of the war, she was assigned to Destroyer Division 3. In April 1942, she was reassigned to conduct operations in northern waters and participated in the invasion of Kiska in June. She was torpedoed and damaged by the American submarine *Thresher* in Makassar Strait on June 27, 1943, and was sunk by the American submarine *Paddle* in the Celebes Sea on July 6, 1944.

Minekaze: She was assigned to the Sasebo Naval District in April 1942 and was active escorting convoys to Saipan, Truk, and Rabaul. Later shifted to escort duties in the East China Sea. On February 10, 1944, she was torpedoed and sunk by the American submarine *Pogy* 85 miles north-northeast of Formosa.

Namikaze: She began the war assigned to Destroyer Division 1 subordinate to the Ominato Guard District. She conducted escort operations in mostly northern waters until being torpedoed on September 8, 1944 in the Kuril Islands. She was moved to Maizuru for conversion into a *kaiten* carrier but saw no action after conversion. She survived the war to be used as a repatriation ship and was given to China in 1947.

Nokaze: She began the war assigned to Destroyer Division 1. She conducted patrol duties in northern waters, including participation in the Aleutians operation in June 1942. She was moved into the South China Sea in January 1945, where she was torpedoed and sunk by the American submarine *Pargo* on February 20, 1945. *Nokaze* was the last destroyer sunk by submarine attack during the war.

Numakaze: At the beginning of the war, she was assigned to Destroyer Division 1. She remained in northern waters until September 1943, conducting general escort duties until transferred for duties in the East China Sea. On December 18, 1943, she was torpedoed and sunk by the American submarine *Grayback*.

Okikaze: She began the war assigned to Ominato Guard District but was reassigned to Yokosuka Naval District in April 1942. She performed escort duties primarily in and near Tokyo Bay. In the course of these duties, she was sunk by the American submarine *Trigger* on January 10, 1943, off Tokyo Bay.

Sawakaze: She began the war assigned to Yokosuka Naval District and was used as an aircraft rescue ship during flight training from carriers. In May 1945 *Sawakaze* was used as a target ship for *kamikaze* training. She survived the war.

Shiokaze: She was assigned to Destroyer Division 3 at the start of the war and participated in the invasion of the southern Philippines. She supported operations in the Dutch East Indies and into the Indian Ocean, escorting the carrier *Ryujo*. She participated in the Aleutian operation in June 1942. She was subsequently transferred to convoy escort duties in August and assigned to southern routes. She surrendered at Kure at the end of the war.

Tachikaze: She was assigned to Destroyer Division 34 at the start of the war. She supported the invasion of the Philippines and later the Dutch East Indies. By July 1942, she had moved to the southwest Pacific to support operations, primarily in the Solomons. She was heavily damaged by an air attack on Rabaul in

This overhead view of a Minekaze-class destroyer clearly shows the layout of ships with its four 4.7in. guns and torpedo battery of three twin mounts. (*Ships of the World*)

Tachikaze being overflown by a F6F-3 Hellcat fighter from Task Force 58 during the massive American carrier raid on Truk. The destroyer had been beached two weeks before the attack and was caught and destroyed on February 17, 1944, with the loss of 67 of her crew. (Naval History and Heritage Command)

December 1942, but was repaired in Japan and returned to Rabaul, where she was twice more damaged by air attack. She was caught at Truk during the massive American carrier air attack on February 17, 1944, and sunk by a torpedo hit aft.

Yakaze: She was assigned to the Kure Naval District at the beginning of the war as a target ship. She surrendered at Yokosuka in a damaged condition in August 1945.

Yukaze: She began the war assigned to Carrier Division 3 and escorted the carrier *Hosho* during the Battle of Midway. She continued to act as plane guard for *Hosho* for pilot training in the Inland Sea until the end of the war. She was used as a repatriation ship after the war, and then handed over to Great Britain and scrapped in 1947.

Minekaze Class Specifications (as completed)	
Displacement	Standard: 1,345 tons / Full Load: 1,650 tons
Dimensions	Length: 336ft 6in. overall / Beam: 30ft / Draft: 9ft 6in.
Speed	39kt
Range	3,600nm at 14kt
Crew	148

KAMIKAZE CLASS

Design and Construction

The second group of Minekaze-class ships was ordered in 1921–22. Because of the differences in design, these were designated as a new class, although these ships were virtually identical to the last three ships of the Minekaze class. Displacement was slightly increased and the greater beam and draft improved stability. This compensated for the increased weight of the modified bridge structure, which now featured a fixed steel covering overhead in place of the previous canvas. The engineering plant was the same, but the increased weight decreased top speed by 2kt.

THE MINEKAZE CLASS

This plate shows three units of the Minekaze class at various points in their careers. The top profile shows *Minekaze* in her pre-war configuration. Clearly evident is the placement of the four single 4.7in. guns and the three twin 21in. torpedo mounts, with the forward mount placed in a well in front of the small bridge structure. The ship is practically devoid of antiaircraft guns. The middle view shows Minekaze-class unit *Yukaze* in 1945. Two of the twin torpedo launchers have been removed, as have two of the 4.7in. guns. In their places are a number of 25mm mounts. Note the increased depth-charge fit on the stern and the No. 13 radar on the foremast. The final view depicts *Namikaze* after conversion into a kaiten carrier in 1945. Most of the original armament has been removed and the stern modified to permit the launch of kaiten manned torpedoes, of which two are shown. Note the No.22 radar on the foremast.

Kamikaze Class Construction				
Ship	Built at	Laid down	Launched	Completed
Kamikaze	Nagasaki by Mitsubishi	12/15/21	09/25/22	12/28/22
Asakaze	Nagasaki by Mitsubishi	02/16/22	12/08/22	06/16/23
Harukaze	Maizuru Navy Yard	05/16/22	12/18/22	05/31/23
Matsukaze	Maizuru Navy Yard	12/02/22	10/30/23	04/05/24
Hatakaze	Maizuru Navy Yard	07/03/23	03/15/24	08/30/24
Oite	Uraga (Tokyo)	03/16/23	11/27/24	10/30/25
Hayate	Ishikawajima (Tokyo)	11/11/22	03/23/25	12/21/25
Asanagi	Fujinagata (Osaka)	03/05/23	04/21/24	12/29/24
Yunagi	Sasebo Navy Yard	09/17/23	04/23/24	04/24/25

Armament and Service Modifications

In terms of the numbers and placement of armament, the Kamikaze-class ships were essentially repeats of the last three ships of the Minekaze class. Torpedo armament was unchanged, but the mounts were now power-operated. The main gun battery was also unchanged and used the same arrangement of the late Minekazes. The anti-aircraft fit was changed to two single 7.7mm machine guns, mounted on each side of the bridge. The last three ships of the class were the first to be equipped with depth charges. These were deployed by two rails on the stern and two single-sided Type 81 depth-charge projectors.

Typical wartime modifications entailed a loss of surface warfare capabilities in exchange for increased anti-aircraft weaponry. This most often included the removal of the aft 4.7in. gun and the aft bank of torpedoes, and the increase of 25mm guns to 10–13in twin and single mounts. As an example, by 1944 *Yunagi* had lost one torpedo mount and two 4.7in. guns, but received four twin and five single 25mm guns. She also received a No. 13 radar on the mainmast. *Kamikaze* and *Harukaze* survived until 1945, and by then each had lost one torpedo mount and their aft 4.7in. gun. In their place, four twin and two single 25mm guns were added. These modifications increased displacement to some 1,523 tons, which brought top speed down to 35kt.

Wartime Service

Asakaze: She was assigned to Destroyer Division 5 at the start of the war and supported the invasions of the Philippines, Malaya, and the Dutch East Indies. She participated in the Battle of Sunda Strait on March 1, 1942, during which the Australian light cruiser *Perth* and American heavy cruiser *Houston* were sunk. She remained active in the southwest area into 1944. While escorting a convoy to Manila, she was torpedoed and sunk by the American submarine *Haddo* west of Lingayen Gulf on August 23, 1944.

Asanagi: She was assigned to Destroyer Division 29 and participated in the capture of the Gilbert Islands in December 1941 and then the second Japanese attempt to take Wake Island on December 23 the same year. She assisted in the invasion of Rabaul in January 1942. After escorting the Lae/Salamua invasion force, she was damaged by an American carrier attack in March. She escorted the Port Moresby invasion convoy in May 1942 during the Battle of the Coral Sea. She subsequently moved to Truk and was sunk by the submarine *Pollack* on May 22, 1944, near the Bonin Islands.

Harukaze: She was assigned to Destroyer Division 5 and supported the advance into the Dutch East Indies. On March 1, 1942, she participated in the Battle of Sunda Strait, where she suffered minor damage. In November 1942, she suffered heavy mine damage off Surabaya. After repairs, she resumed escort duties in the central Pacific. In November 1944, she was torpedoed and damaged by the submarine *Sailfish* in the Luzon Strait. She was later damaged by a carrier air attack in January 1945, which forced a return to Japan where she was surrendered, unrepaired, at the end of the war.

Hatakaze: She began the war assigned to Destroyer Division 5, and was active in this division into March 1942. In May 1942, she was assigned to the Yokosuka Naval District and assumed escort duties from there. In December 1944, she was reassigned to duties in the East China Sea. On January 15, 1945, she was sunk by an American air attack in Takao, Formosa.

Hayate: As part of Destroyer Division 29, she became the first Japanese destroyer lost in the war when, on December 11, 1941, 5in. shore batteries on Wake Island probably hit her torpedo tubes, creating a large explosion that quickly sank the ship, with no survivors.

Kamikaze: She was assigned to Destroyer Division 1, which was subordinate to the Ominato Guard District, with the three late units of the Minekaze class. She spent almost the entire war active in northern waters. In January 1945, she moved to the South China Sea. In May 1945, she escorted the heavy cruiser *Haguro* on a mission to the Andaman Islands. British destroyers sank the *Haguro* and damaged the *Kamikaze*. In June, she escorted the heavy cruiser *Ashigara*, which was sunk by a British submarine attack. She survived the war and was surrendered in Singapore in August 1945, and then used as a repatriation ship.

Matsukaze: She began the war assigned to Destroyer Division 5 and acted as other ships of that division during the first period of the war. In June 1943, she was assigned to duties operating from Rabaul and was active conducting multiple transport runs to islands in the Central and Northern Solomons area. She was caught in Truk in February 1944 during an American carrier air attack and suffered moderate damage. On June 9, 1944, she was sunk by the American submarine *Swordfish* near the Bonin Islands.

Oite: She was assigned to Destroyer Division 29 at the start of the war. She participated in the initial unsuccessful Japanese invasion of Wake Island on December 11, 1941, where she was damaged by gunfire from Marine coastal batteries. She took part in the successful attempt to seize the island on December 23. She also assisted in invasion of Rabaul in January and Lae/Salamua in March 1942. During the Battle of Coral Sea, she escorted the Port Moresby invasion convoy. Operating out of Rabaul, she made several transport runs, including to Guadalcanal. Later she moved to Truk to assume escort duties. During the American carrier air attack on Truk on February 18, she was hit and sunk by an air-launched torpedo.

Yunagi: She was assigned to Destroyer Division 29 at the start of the war and participated in the December 1941 invasion of the Gilbert Islands and then the second attempt to capture Wake Island on December 23. She participated in the invasion of Rabaul in January 1942. In March, she was assigned to the Lae/Salamua invasion force, but suffered moderate damage as a result of American carrier air attacks on March 10, which forced a return to Japan for repairs.

The Kamikaze class was a virtual repeat of the last three units of the preceding Minekaze class, as shown by this 1936 view of *Kamikaze*. Like the Minekaze class, the Kamikaze class was obsolescent by the start of the war and was assigned secondary duties. (Yamato Museum)

She returned to Rabaul in time to participate in the Battle of Savo Island on August 9, 1942. From Rabaul, she engaged in multiple transport runs. On July 5, 1943, one of these resulted in an engagement off New Georgia Island. A Japanese torpedo barrage, including weapons from *Yunagi*, sank an American destroyer, with no Japanese losses. Days later, on July 13, *Yunagi* participated in the Battle of Kolombangara. After Japanese units withdrew from the Solomons, she assumed escort duties in the central Pacific. She participated in the Battle of the Philippine Sea in June 1944. On August 25, while escorting a convoy to Manila, she was torpedoed and sunk by the American submarine *Picuda*.

This close-up 1936 view of *Yunagi* shows the modified bridge structure of this class and the turtleback characteristic of the forecastle. *Yunagi* went on to have a fine war record. (Yamato Museum)

Kamikaze Class Specifications (as completed)

Displacement	Standard: 1,400 tons / Full Load: 1,720 tons
Dimensions	Length: 336ft 6in. overall / Beam: 30ft / Draft: 10ft
Speed	37kt
Range	3,600nm at 14kt
Crew	148

MUTSUKI CLASS

Design and Construction

The 12 ships of the Mutsuki class were ordered as part of the 1923 program. As was standard with the previous two classes of first-class destroyers, the new ships were completed with numbers only; names were not given until 1928.

Mutsuki Class Construction

Ship	Built at	Laid down	Launched	Completed
Mutsuki	Sasebo Naval Yard	05/21/24	07/23/25	03/25/26
Kisaragi	Maizuru Navy Yard	06/03/24	06/05/25	12/25/25
Yayoi	Uraga (Tokyo)	01/11/24	07/11/25	08/28/26
Uzuki	Ishikawajima (Tokyo)	01/11/24	10/15/25	09/14/26
Satsuki	Fujinagata (Osaka)	12/01/23	03/25/25	11/15/25
Minazuki	Uraga (Tokyo)	03/24/25	05/25/26	03/22/27
Fumizuki	Fujinagata (Osaka)	10/20/24	02/16/26	07/03/26
Nagatsuki	Ishikawajima (Tokyo)	04/16/25	10/06/26	04/30/27
Kikuzuki	Maizuru Navy Yard	06/15/25	05/15/26	11/20/26
Mikazuki	Sasebo Navy Yard	08/21/25	07/12/26	05/07/27
Mochizuki	Uraga (Tokyo)	03/23/26	04/28/27	10/31/27
Yuzuki	Fujinagata (Osaka)	11/27/26	03/04/27	07/25/27

In most respects, the Mutsuki class was identical to the Kamikaze class. However, the Mutsuki class did introduce several new features and clearly demonstrated the Japanese predilection for a heavy torpedo armament. These were the first destroyers built under the Washington Naval Treaty. While this treaty did not restrict destroyer numbers or design directly, it did force the Imperial Navy to accept inferiority in capital ships. In an effort to compensate for this weakness, the Japanese attempted to arm other types of ships as heavily as possible. This trend was immediately observable with the new Mutsuki design, which was given a heavier torpedo armament in order to threaten capital ships.

In addition to the difference in the torpedo armament, the principal difference in appearance was the adoption of an S-shaped bow, which had a more prominent flare and provided improved seaworthiness. This also resulted in a slightly greater length, which slightly increased displacement. Machinery was the same as on the Kamikaze class, with the exception of two ships that received foreign-made turbines. Full-load speed for the class was disappointing and barely exceeded 33kt.

Armament and Service Modifications

The biggest difference in the Mutsuki class was the alteration of the torpedo armament. For the first time on a Japanese destroyer, 24in. tubes were fitted. The Mutsuki-class ships carried six 24in. tubes in two triple launchers. Though unworkable in heavy seas, a mount was still placed in the well position forward of the bridge. Use of triple mounts instead of the previous twin torpedo mounts provided more deck space and a more attractive overall design. For the first time, spare torpedoes were provided, with each tube having a reload. Gun armament remained unaltered at four 4.7in. single mounts arranged in a similar fashion to the Kamikaze class. Two 7.7mm machine guns were placed abreast the bridge for anti-aircraft protection. Anti-submarine armament included two stern depth-charge racks and two Type 81 projectors. A total of 18 depth charges were carried. Before the war, units in the class received shields for the torpedo mounts, and the two stacks were raked. Wartime modifications commenced soon after the war began, and centered on augmenting the ships' anti-aircraft fit. Some ships immediately received additional twin 13mm machine guns forward of the bridge and abaft the aft stack. In 1942, *Mikazuki* had a boiler removed and her aft stack was reduced in size – she was the only ship of the class so modified. *Yayoi* had a similar reduction to her forward funnel; again, she was the only ship of the class so adapted. Between September 1942 and December 1943, *Uzuki* had her stern modified to facilitate the launching and recovery of landing barges. She was the only ship of the class to be modified as a destroyer transport.

There was no standard modification for the class during the second half of the war. Those ships surviving into 1943 began to lose one or two of their 4.7in. guns, and four units had their aft bank of torpedo tubes removed. This provided more deck space for cargo and reduced top weight. The three ships that survived into the second half of 1944, *Uzuki*, *Satsuki*, and *Yuzuki*, were further modified and received between 16 and 22 25mm guns.

Satsuki was the first unit to get radar, which did not occur until February–March 1944. Only two other units received radar and these were the No. 13 set fitted on the mainmast.

Wartime Service

Fumizuki: She began the war assigned to Destroyer Division 22 and supported the invasion of the Philippines and the Dutch East Indies during first phase of the war. In January 1943 she moved to Rabaul and supported three evacuation runs from Guadalcanal in February. She remained based at Rabaul and conducted several transport runs to points on New Britain and in the Solomons. She suffered minor damage from air attack on Rabaul on November 2, 1943, and again on January 4, 1944. She was caught in Truk on February 17, 1944. A single torpedo hit caused gradual flooding, which sank the ship the next day.

Kikuzuki: She began the war assigned to Destroyer Division 23 and participated in the invasion of Guam in December 1941, followed by the invasion of Rabaul in January 1942. She supported the Lae/Salamua operation in March.

Mutsuki on her launch day, July 23, 1925. Carrying 24in. torpedoes, the Mutsuki-class ships were considered to be front-line units by the Japanese and were heavily committed to the Solomons campaign. (Yamato Museum)

In May, she was assigned to the Tulagi invasion force. An American carrier air attack caught *Kikusuki* in Tulagi Harbor on May 4, 1942, and hit her with one torpedo. The ship was beached, but sank the next day.

Kisaragi: The ship was assigned to Destroyer Division 30 at the commencement of war. In the first attempt to seize Wake Island on December 11, 1941, she was hit by bombs from aircraft. The crew was unable to put out the fires, and the ship suddenly blew up and sank with the loss of all aboard.

Mikazuki: She began the war assigned to Carrier Division 3 to perform plane guard duties for carriers *Hosho* and *Zuiho* in home waters. In June 1942 she escorted *Zuiho* during the Battle of Midway. After modification between March and June 1943, she was assigned to operate from Rabaul. She was present at the battles of Kula Gulf and Kolombangara in July 1943. She grounded on a reef near Cape Gloucester on July 27, and was sunk the next day by B-25 bombers.

Minazuki: She began the war assigned to Destroyer Division 22 and supported the invasions of the Philippines and the Dutch East Indies, remaining in the southern areas until early 1943. After moving to Rabaul, she conducted a series of transport runs, mostly in the Central and Northern Solomons. She was damaged in July by air attack. She escorted the final convoy into Rabaul in February 1944. On June 6, 1944, she was sunk by the American submarine *Harder* off Tawi-Tawi.

Mochizuki: She was assigned to Destroyer Division 30 at the start of the war, and took part in the two operations against Wake Island in December 1941. She participated in the January 1942 capture of Rabaul, the March 1942 landings at Lae/Salamua, and the Battle of the Coral Sea in May. Operating from Rabaul, she participated in the October 15 bombardment of Henderson Field on Guadalcanal, followed by three troop transport runs to the island. She escorted the important mid-November 1942 troop convoy to Guadalcanal, and participated in the Battle of Kula Gulf on July 5–6, 1943. On a transport run on October 24, 1943, she was attacked by American aircraft and sunk by a bomb hit in the engineering space, 90 miles south-southwest of Rabaul.

Mutsuki: She began the war assigned to Destroyer Division 30 and participated in the two December 1941 Wake Island operations, followed by the invasion of Rabaul in January 1942 and the invasion of Lae/Salamua in March. She took part in the Battle of the Coral Sea as an escort to the main invasion convoy. Between June 25 and July 1, she escorted the lead echelon of airfield construction crews to Guadalcanal. After the American seizure of the airfield, she conducted a

B   **YUNAGI AT THE BATTLE OF SAVO ISLAND, AUGUST 1942**

Yunagi was the only Kamikaze-class ship to engage in surface combat with Allied forces during the war. Compared to the earlier Minekaze class, the bridge structure has been modified and the placement of the two aft 4.7in. guns altered. At Savo Island, *Yunagi* was placed at the rear of the Japanese column. Early in the battle she was directed to leave the column and soon attracted the attention of the American heavy cruiser Chicago. *Yunagi* claimed this ship as sunk, and then engaged American destroyer *Jarvis* a few minutes later in a private duel, as shown in this scene. *Yunagi* retired, undamaged, with the Japanese force after it had sunk four Allied heavy cruisers.

A fine beam shot of *Minazuki* in March 1927. The view clearly shows the main battery of four 4.7in. guns and the forward torpedo mount in the well deck forward of the bridge. The torpedo mounts were provided with shields before the war. (Yamato Museum)

bombardment of Henderson Field on August 24. On the next day, she was hit by a B-17 bomber 40 miles northeast of Santa Isabel Island during the Battle of the Eastern Solomons and sunk.

Nagatsuki: She began the war assigned to Destroyer Division 22 and participated in the landings on the Philippines and later in Malaya and the Dutch East Indies. She moved to the Rabaul area in January 1943 and participated in the evacuation of Guadalcanal in February. Operating from Rabaul, she made transport runs throughout the Solomons. In a battle off New Georgia Island on July 4–5, she participated in the sinking of American destroyer *Strong*. She was subsequently sunk on July 6, 1943, after running aground on Kolombangara Island during the Battle of Kula Gulf, and was finished off the same day by American aircraft.

Satsuki: She began the war assigned to Destroyer Division 22 and participated in the landings on the Philippines, Malaya, and the Dutch East Indies. She moved to the Rabaul area in January 1943 and participated in the evacuation of Guadalcanal on February 1, 4, and 7. She remained active out of Rabaul and participated in the battles of Kula Gulf and Kolombangara in July. In 1944, she conducted escort missions in the central Pacific and the South China Sea. On September 21, she was caught by an American carrier aircraft in Manila Harbor and sunk by three bomb hits.

Uzuki: She began the war assigned to Carrier Division 2. Her first action was the seizure of Guam in December 1941; this was followed by the occupation of Kavieng in January 1942, the Lae/Salamua operation in March, and the Coral Sea operation in May. In late June and early July, she escorted a convoy with construction troops to Guadalcanal. She participated in the Battle of the Eastern Solomons and was lightly damaged by a B-17 bomber attack. Following alteration in Japan into a destroyer-transport, she returned to Rabaul by December 1942 and was heavily damaged that month in a collision with a transport. She returned to action to conduct several transport runs in the Northern Solomons. On November 24–25, 1943, she was involved in the Battle of Cape St George, where three of the five Japanese destroyers were sunk. She participated in the Battle of the Philippine Sea in June 1944. As part of the large-scale Japanese efforts to reinforce the island of Leyte in the Philippines, she was torpedoed and sunk by two American PT boats on December 12, 1944, 50 miles northeast of Cebu.

Yayoi: She was assigned to Destroyer Division 30 at the start of the war and participated in the failed invasion of Wake Island on December 11, 1941, where she suffered minor damage from an American shore battery. She was present at the successful invasion of Wake Island on December 23, the invasion of Rabaul in January 1942, the Lae/Salamua invasion in March, and the Battle of the Coral Sea in May. She was active in support of operations off Guadalcanal, including the Battle of the Eastern Solomons on August 25, 1942. She was sunk by air attack on September 11 northwest of Vakuta Island.

Fumizuki under attack from the light carrier *Monterey*'s aircraft on January 4, 1944, off Kavieng. The ship was only lightly damaged in this attack, but was sunk the next month at Truk by a single torpedo, with the loss of 29 crewmen. (Naval History and Heritage Command)

Yuzuki: She began the war assigned to Destroyer Division 23. She participated in invasions of Guam, Kavieng, and Lae/Salamua. She was damaged by air attack following the May 3, 1942 invasion of Tulagi, but remained active from Rabaul until February 1944. Following the Battle of Leyte Gulf, she was assigned to escort convoys from Manila to Leyte. She was sunk by American aircraft 65 miles north-northeast of Cebu on December 12, 1944.

Mutsuki Class Specifications (as completed)	
Displacement	Standard: 1,315 tons / Full load: 1,772 tons
Dimensions	Length: 336ft overall / Beam: 30ft / Draft: 10ft
Speed	37kt (design), 33.5kt in service
Range	4,000nm at 14kt
Crew	150

FUBUKI CLASS

Design and Construction

The Fubuki class was the most important and influential Japanese destroyer class. Commissioned beginning in 1928, they were at the time the most powerful destroyers in the world, being some ten years ahead of their time in their design. Several new features were introduced, which became standard on future destroyers. They surpassed the firepower of the Imperial Navy's light cruisers and remained valuable units up through the Pacific War.

The effect of the 1922 Washington Naval Treaty on Japanese destroyer design was fully realized in the Fubuki class. Locked into a position of inferiority regarding capital ships, the Japanese sought other ways to redress the balance. The obvious answer was to build other types of ships not restricted by naval treaties and arm them as powerfully as possible. Design work for the new class of destroyer began as early as October 1922 with a proposal for a large 2,000-ton design, which would provide the endurance necessary for long-range Pacific operations, the space for a heavy armament, and machinery for high speeds. Eventually, it was decided to approve a smaller 1,750-ton design, but this was only on the condition that no loss of firepower occurred.

Fubuki Class (Special Type) Construction

Ship	Built at	Laid down	Launched	Completed
*Fubuki**	Maizuru Navy Yard	06/16/26	11/15/27	08/10/28
*Shirayuki**	Yokohama	03/19/27	03/20/28	12/18/28
*Hatsuyuki**	Maizuru Navy Yard	04/12/27	09/29/28	03/30/29
*Miyuki**	Uraga	04/30/27	06/26/28	06/29/29
*Murakumo**	Fujinagata (Osaka)	04/25/27	09/27/28	05/10/29
*Shinonome**	Sasebo Naval Shipyard	08/12/26	11/26/27	05/27/28
*Usugumo**	Ishikawajima (Tokyo)	10/21/26	12/26/27	07/26/28
*Shirakumo**	Fujinagata (Osaka)	10/27/26	12/27/27	07/28/28
*Isonami**	Uraga	10/18/26	11/24/27	06/30/28
*Uranami**	Sasebo Naval Shipyard	04/28/27	11/29/28	06/30/29
Ayanami	Fujinagata (Osaka)	01/20/28	10/05/29	04/30/30
Shikinami	Maizuru Navy Yard	07/06/28	06/22/29	12/24/29
Asagiri	Sasebo Naval Shipyard	12/12/28	11/18/29	06/30/30
Yugiri	Maizuru Navy Yard	04/01/29	05/12/30	12/03/30
Amagiri	Ishikawajima (Tokyo)	11/28/28	02/27/30	11/10/30
Sagiri	Uraga	03/28/29	12/23/29	01/31/31
Oboro	Sasebo Naval Shipyard	11/29/29	11/08/30	10/31/31
Akebono	Fujinagata (Osaka)	10/25/29	11/07/30	07/31/31
Sazanami	Maizuru Navy Yard	02/21/30	06/06/31	05/19/32
Ushio	Uraga	12/24/29	11/17/30	11/14/31

*Indicates Group I, all others are Group II

Several modifications took place over the course of production, and the 24 units of the Special Type (as they were also known) broke down into three groups. The final four ships were so different they were given a new class name.

The power of the machinery was increased to 50,000 SHP, developed by four boilers driving two geared turbines. This translated into a top speed of 35kt. Increased bunkerage also increased the type's range to 5,000nm. The ventilation ducts to the boiler rooms were of different designs and provided another way to distinguish Group I units from Group II. The first nine ships had massive air ducts abreast the two stacks. The last ship of Group I, *Uranami*, dispensed with the large air ducts and adopted the new design of integrating the ventilation ducts into the platforms built around the stacks. The stacks of Group I ships were circular, while ships from Group II had rectangular-shaped stacks. All ships of Group II adopted the modified ventilation system introduced on *Uranami* and the new type of stacks.

The design of the hull also increased seaworthiness. The removal of the well deck in front of the bridge made it possible to extend the forecastle further aft. The forecastle was raised one deck in an effort to reduce the effect of heavy seas on the forward gun mount and the bridge. The S-shaped curved bow introduced on the Mutsuki class was retained. The flare of the bow was increased, and the hull back to the first stack was flared to some degree to enhance seaworthiness.

C — **THE MUTSUKI AND FUBUKI CLASSES**

The top and middle views in this plate show Mutsuki-class *Satsuki* as she appeared in 1944, with her augmented antiaircraft and radar fit. Several differences from the earlier Minekaze and Kamikaze classes are evident, including the S-shaped bow, the larger bridge structure, and the shielded 24in. torpedo mounts. The overhead view shows the differences from the early-war appearance of the Mutsuki class. The aft 4.7in. gun has been removed and replaced with two triple 25mm mounts. Note the No. 13 radar on the mainmast. The bottom view depicts Special Type destroyer *Fubuki* as she was built in 1928. *Fubuki* was a Group I Special Type unit, as can be discerned by the Type A 5in. gun mounts and the prominent air intakes for the boiler rooms.

Mikatsuki under attack from US Army Air Force B-25 bombers after running aground near Cape Gloucester on July 28, 1943, on a troop transport run to Tuvulu on New Britain. (Naval History and Heritage Command)

The bridge was much larger than on previous classes, since greater height was required to clear the large 5in. mount placed forward. The bridge was completely covered and given glass windows. On Group II ships, the bridge was given another level.

What emerged in 1928 with the commissioning of *Fubuki* was a very impressive ship. However, despite the extensive design features employed to reduce weight, including use of welding on the hull and lighter alloys above the main deck, the ships were some 200 tons over their design weight. The overweight issue was even more of a problem with the Group II ships, which had the larger bridge and the heavier Type B gun mounts. Soon after entering service, the ships received shields for the three torpedo mounts, further increasing top weight.

The result of this was a serious stability problem. The first sign of trouble occurred in March 1934, when a torpedo boat employing some of the same design principles as the Special Type destroyers capsized in heavy weather. An investigation revealed the problem to be excessive top weight, but before any modifications could be considered for the Special Type destroyers, disaster struck. On September 26, 1935, while on exercises east of Japan, the fleet ran into a typhoon. Two Special Type destroyers lost their bows in the storm, another three received severe structural damage, and another six experienced some hull damage. As a result, the entire class returned to the yards in November 1935–38 for hull strengthening and top weight reduction. A ballast keel and 40 extra tons of ballast were added. The large bridge structure was reduced in size and the height of the stacks decreased. Magazine stowage was lessened and the number of torpedo reloads was reduced from nine to three (for the center torpedo mount only). Eight of the Group II units received the lighter Type C 5in. mount. Bunkerage was increased to create more weight down in the hull. The net result was to increase overall displacement to 2,090 tons, which in turn reduced maximum speed to 34kt.

Armament and Service Modifications

The armament of the Special Type destroyers was their most important feature. The ships gained a 50 percent increase over the previous Mutsuki class in both gunnery and torpedo power. The new 24in. torpedoes had proved entirely satisfactory on the Mutsuki class, and these were again used on the Special Type ships. Each had three triple-torpedo mounts and each tube was given a reload for an impressive total of 18 torpedoes.

The main gun armament was increased to a 5in. weapon. Six of these were carried in three twin mounts. For the first time on a destroyer these were provided with a weatherproof gun house with a 3mm thick shield. These gun houses provided no protection against shells or even bullets, and only a bare degree of protection from shrapnel (making them mounts, not turrets). Group I units had the Type A 5in. mount with a 40 degree elevation, making them suitable for low angle targets only. Group II ships were given the Type B mount. The original anti-aircraft fit was a pair of 7.7mm machine guns fitted in front of the second stack.

After their reconstruction, the ships were little modified until the start of the war. By then, the anti-aircraft armament was a meager one or two 13mm twin mounts located in front of the second funnel.

Wartime modifications focused on the augmentation of the anti-aircraft fit. The first step was to fit selected units with a twin 13mm mount in front of the bridge. These 13mm mounts were eventually exchanged for twin 25mm mounts on most units. With the increasing American air threat, the Japanese began to take protection from air attack more seriously. By late 1943 and into 1944, this meant removal of one of the aft 5in. mounts and replacement with two triple 25mm mounts on surviving Special Type units. Another raised gun position was built between the two aft torpedo mounts, which provided room for another two triple 25mm mounts. In the later part of 1944, the few units still afloat received additional 25mm guns in the form of single mounts usually positioned on the forecastle and near the stern. As many as 15 were carried in this manner. Some units also received single 13mm mounts.

The first unit to receive radar was *Yugiri*, which received a No. 22 set by November 1943. A total of seven ships received the No. 22 set, which was positioned on a rebuilt tripod mast above the bridge. Those few units surviving late into 1944 also received the No. 13 radar, which was added to the mainmast aft.

Wartime Service

Akebono: She began the war assigned to Destroyer Division 7 and participated in the invasions of the southern Philippines and the Dutch East Indies. She engaged in the March 1, 1942 action, in which the British heavy cruiser *Exeter* and an American and British destroyer were sunk by torpedoes and gunfire. In May 1942, she participated in the Battle of the Coral Sea as an escort to the Japanese carrier force. In June, she was involved in the Aleutians operation. She conducted escort operations in the Central Pacific throughout 1943 and into 1944. During the Battle of Leyte Gulf in October 1944, she was assigned as part of the 2nd Diversion Attack Force and participated in the later stages of the Battle of Surigao Strait. On November 5, she was heavily damaged by an American air raid on Manila Harbor, and was sunk in a subsequent raid on November 13.

Amagiri: One of the most active Special Type units and arguably the most famous, as she destroyed the PT boat commanded by future American president John F. Kennedy. She began the war assigned to Destroyer Division 20 and participated in the invasions of Malaya, Sumatra, and the Andaman Islands in the Indian Ocean. She also participated in the April 1942 raid into the Indian Ocean, assisting in the sinking of three Allied merchant ships. She participated in the

Nagatsuki grounded on Kolombangara Island on May 8, 1944. The ship had been beached during the Battle of Kula Gulf on July 6, 1943, and was later bombed by US Army Air Force aircraft. Only eight crewmen died, with the others reaching safety over land. (Naval History and Heritage Command)

Midway operation as part of the Aleutians Guard Force. She moved into the South Pacific in August in response to the American seizure of Guadalcanal in the Solomon Islands. Operating out of Rabaul, she conducted five transport missions and three sweep missions in the waters off Guadalcanal, as well as some 20 other missions to points in the Solomons before returning to Japan for refit. In 1943, she participated in the Battle of Kula Gulf on July 5–6 and survived the Battle of Cape St George in November, where American destroyers sank three of five Japanese destroyers present. While conducting missions in the central Solomons, she rammed and sank PT-109 on August 2, 1943. In March 1944, she was assigned to the Southwest Area Fleet and was sunk by a mine in the Makassar Strait on April 23, 1944.

Asagiri: She began the war assigned to Destroyer Division 20. She participated in the invasion of Malaya and, on January 27, 1942, assisted in the sinking of the British destroyer *Thanet* off Endau. Later she covered the invasion of Sumatra and the Andaman Islands. In April, she moved into the Indian Ocean and assisted in the sinking of six merchant ships. She participated in the Midway operation as part of the Aleutians Guard Force. On her first transport run to Guadalcanal, she was sunk by air attack on August 28, 1942, 60 miles north-northeast of Savo Island.

Ayanami: She began the war assigned to Destroyer Division 19 and participated in the invasions of Malaya, Sumatra, and the Andaman Islands. She was involved in the Midway operation as part of the main body. She began the first of seven transport runs to Guadalcanal in October 1942. She was sunk during the Second Naval Battle of Guadalcanal on November 14–15 by 5in. guns from the American battleship *Washington* southeast of Savo Island.

Fubuki: She began the war assigned to Destroyer Division 11 and supported the invasions of Malaya, British Borneo, and the Anambas Islands during the first two months of the war. She was subsequently assigned to support the invasion of the Dutch East Indies in February 1942, and participated in the Battle of Sunda Strait. She moved into the Indian Ocean in March to cover the invasion of the Andaman Islands. She participated in the Battle of Midway in June. She moved to the South Pacific, arriving at Rabaul in late August 1942, and conducted 11 transport or sweep missions to waters off Guadalcanal. She was sunk on October 11, 1942 in the Battle of Cape Esperance by American cruiser gunfire. Unusually, 109 of her crew were saved by American ships.

Hatsuyuki: The ship began the war assigned to Destroyer Division 11 and mirrored the activity of *Fubuki* (with the exception of suffering minor damage at Sunda Strait) through August 1942. Activity off Guadalcanal included five transport missions (during one, two American destroyer transports were sunk on September 5) and four sweep missions, including the Battle of Cape Esperance and the Second Naval Battle of Guadalcanal. She returned to Rabaul in June 1943 and conducted four missions in the Solomons before participating in the Battle of Kula Gulf on July 6, where she was damaged by three dud shells. She was sunk by air attack in Shortlands Harbor on July 17, 1943.

Isonami: She was assigned to Destroyer Division 19 and escorted Malaya invasion convoys, later participating in the invasion of the Dutch East Indies in February 1942. In March, she formed part of the Andaman Islands invasion force. She was part of the main body during the Midway operations in June. She did not reach Rabaul until November 1942. She conducted four transport runs to points on New Guinea into December, then two transport operations in the Solomons, including one to Guadalcanal. She was sunk by the American submarine *Tautog* on April 9, 1943 after departing from Surabaya.

Murakumo: She was assigned to Destroyer Division 12 with *Shirakumo* and *Shinonome*. During the first period of the war, she escorted invasion convoys to Malaya, British Borneo, and then the Dutch East Indies. She participated in the Battle of Sunda Strait on March 1, 1942. In March, she covered the invasion of Sumatra and the Andaman Islands in the Indian Ocean. She was assigned to the main body for the June 1942 Midway operation. She arrived in Rabaul in late August and conducted ten transport missions (eight to Guadalcanal) and two sweep missions. On her last transport run on October 12, 1942, she was sunk by air attack 90 miles northwest of Savo Island.

Oboro: The ship began war assigned to Carrier Division 5 and participated in the Japanese seizure of Guam in December 1941. While conducting a transport run to Kiska Island in the Aleutians, she was sunk by B-26 air attack on October 16, 1942.

Sagiri: She was assigned to Destroyer Division 20 at the start of the war. While providing escort for the invasion of British Borneo, she was sunk by the Dutch submarine *K-XVI* off Sarawak on December 24, 1941.

Sazanami: She began the war assigned to Destroyer Division 7. She was assigned with *Ushio* to bombard Midway Atoll on December 7, 1941. Later she assisted in the invasion of the Dutch East Indies and saw action in the Battle of the Java Sea on February 27, 1942. She participated in the Coral Sea operation in May and the Midway operation in June 1942. In September, she began operations off Guadalcanal, conducting three transport runs and one sweep mission. In August 1943, she was made flagship of Destroyer Squadron 3 and saw action in the Battle off Horaniu that month. After departing Rabaul, she was sunk by the American submarine *Albacore* on January 14, 1944.

Shikinami: She began the war assigned to Destroyer Division 19 and participated in the invasion of Malaya. During the Battle of Sunda Strait on February 28–March 1, she finished off the American heavy cruiser *Houston* with a Type 90 torpedo. She was involved in the Midway operation as part of the main body. She moved to the South Pacific and participated in the Battle of the Eastern Solomons in August 1942, later moving to Rabaul. From there, she conducted 11 transport missions and three sweep mission to waters off Guadalcanal, participating in the Second Naval Battle of Guadalcanal on November 14–15.

LEFT
Shirayuki in May 1929. She was a Group I Special Type unit. Prominent recognition features for Group I units include the Type A 5in. guns, round stacks, and the large air intakes for the boiler rooms, all clearly seen in this view. (Yamato Museum)

RIGHT
Uranami was a transition unit between Group I and Group II Special Type destroyers. As the last of the Group I units, she still has Type A 5in. mounts, but has the stacks and modified air intakes found on Group II units. (Yamato Museum)

Akebono in July 1936 before she returned to the yards for reconstruction work that would reduce the size of the bridge structure and the height of the stacks. Note that all the torpedo mounts are equipped with shields. (Yamato Museum)

In March 1943, she was assigned as part of an escort for a troop convoy from Rabaul to New Guinea, and survived Allied air attacks during the Battle of the Bismarck Sea. Subsequently she was assigned to the Southwest Area Fleet. She participated in the abortive troop reinforcement operation at Biak on June 1944 and incurred slight damage due to air attack. She was sunk on September 12 by the American submarine *Growler* south of Hong Kong.

Shinonome: The ship was assigned to Destroyer Division 12, and was sunk by two bombs from a Dutch flying boat on December 18, 1941, off Borneo.

Shirakumo: She was assigned to Destroyer Division 12 and escorted invasion convoys to Malaya, British Borneo, and then the Dutch East Indies. She participated in the Battle of Sunda Strait on March 1, 1942, in which she and *Murakumo* destroyed a Dutch destroyer. In March, she escorted the invasions of Sumatra and the Andaman Islands. She participated in the April Indian Ocean raid and assisted in the destruction of five Allied merchant ships. She was assigned to the Aleutians Guard Force for the Midway operation. In late August, she was hit by American dive bombers on her first transport run to Guadalcanal and forced to return to Japan for repairs. In April 1943, she began operations in northern waters until she was sunk on March 16, 1944, by the American submarine *Tautog*.

Shirayuki: With *Fubuki* and *Hatsuyuki*, she was assigned to Destroyer Division 11 and mirrored their activity through August 1942. She was very active off Guadalcanal, conducting a total of five sweep missions (including the Second Naval Battle of Guadalcanal on November 15) and 13 transport missions. She participated in the three evacuation missions from Guadalcanal in February 1943. She was sunk by skip-bombing on March 3, 1943, during the Battle of the Bismarck Sea.

Uranami: She began the war assigned to Destroyer Division 19. While escorting a Malaya invasion convoy, she sank Dutch submarine *O-20* on December 19, 1941. Beginning in late February 1942, she participated in the invasion of the Dutch East Indies and in March covered the invasion of the Andaman Islands in Indian Ocean. She was involved in the Midway operation as part of the main body. She moved to the South Pacific and participated in the Battle of the Eastern Solomons in August, later moving to Rabaul. Operating out of Rabaul, she conducted 12 transport missions and five sweep mission to waters off Guadalcanal; she participated in the Second Naval Battle of Guadalcanal on November 14–15. In March 1943, she was assigned as part of the escort for a troop convoy from Rabaul to New Guinea, and survived Allied air attacks during the Battle of the Bismarck Sea. Subsequently she was assigned to the Southwest Area Fleet. She participated in the abortive troop reinforcement operation at Biak in June 1944. During the Battle of Leyte Gulf, she was sunk by American escort carrier attack on October 26 north-northeast of Panay Island.

Ushio: The only Fubuki-class unit to survive the war. She began the war assigned to Destroyer Division 7 and bombarded Midway on December 7, 1941. She participated in the invasion of the Dutch East Indies and the Battle of the Java Sea on February 27, 1942. With *Sazanami*, she depth-charged and sank the American submarine *Perch* on March 3, 1942. She was involved in the Battle of the Coral Sea as part of the Carrier Striking Force and in the Midway operation as part of the carrier force tasked to cover the Aleutians invasion. She participated in the Battle of the Eastern

Looking aft from the bridge of a Group II Special Type destroyer, from where the fine lines of the ship are evident. The deck is covered in linoleum strips. Note the 13mm gun position located forward of the second stack. (*Ships of the World*)

Ayanami pictured on April 30, 1930, the day the ship was commissioned. The size of the bridge structure was later reduced as part of the reconstruction to reduce top weight. *Ayanami* was one of the first Group II units, and was also one of the first Special Type units lost during the war. (Yamato Museum)

Solomons in August 1942. Later she conducted three transport runs and one sweep mission to Guadalcanal. She was tasked with Central Pacific escort operations in 1943 and into 1944. For the Battle of Leyte Gulf, she was assigned to the 2nd Diversion Attack Force and saw action at the Battle of Surigao Strait in October. Later she escorted several troop convoys from Manila to Ormoc on Leyte. She was damaged in an air attack on Manila in November 1944 and eventually returned to Japan. She surrendered, unrepaired, at end of war.

Usugumo: This ship was the only destroyer not ready for combat operations at the start of the war, since she had struck a mine off China in August 1940. Repairs were completed in July 1942 and she was assigned duties in northern waters. She was present at the Battle of the Komandorski Islands in March 1943, but not involved. She participated in the evacuation of Kiska in July–August 1943. She remained in northern waters until July 7, 1944 when she was sunk by the American submarine *Skate* in the Sea of Okhotsk.

Yugiri: She began the war assigned to Destroyer Division 20. She participated in the invasions of Malaya and the sinking of the British destroyer *Thanet* off Endau on January 27, 1942. In March, she covered invasions of Sumatra and the Andaman Islands and participated in the Indian Ocean raid in April. She was involved in the Midway operation as part of the Aleutians Guard Force. In her first transport operation to Guadalcanal, she was hit by an American bomb on August 28 and forced to return to Japan for repairs. She returned to Rabaul in January 1943. On her fifth mission out of Rabaul, she was torpedoed by the American submarine *Grayback* northwest of Kavieng and heavily damaged, and was again forced to return to Japan for repairs. She returned to Rabaul in November 1943, and was sunk at the Battle of Cape St George on November 25 by American destroyer gunfire.

Shinonome was a Group I Special Type unit. She was the first Special Type destroyer lost in the war, being bombed by Dutch aircraft in December 1941. A magazine explosion resulted in the loss of her entire crew. (Naval History and Heritage Command)

D *Hatsuyuki* as she appeared during the Battle of Cape Esperance in October 1942. This plate shows the Group II Special Type destroyer in its early-war configuration. The Group II ship can be distinguished from the Group I units by its Type B 5in. gun mounts and the lack of large air intakes. Aside from the addition of a twin 13mm mount in front of the bridge, *Hatsuyuki* remained in this configuration until sunk in July 1943.

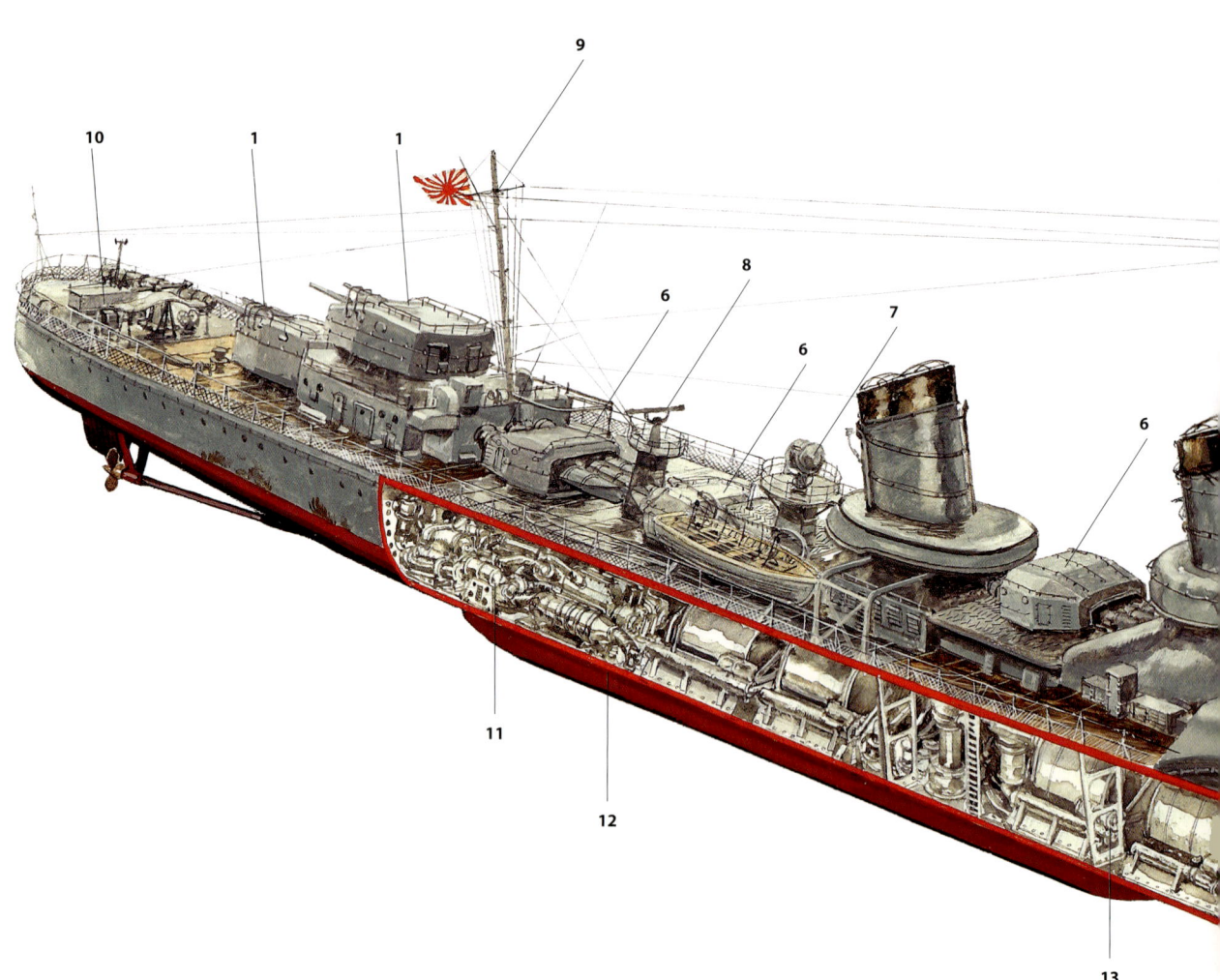

Key

1. Type B 5in. gun mount (3)
2. Compass bridge
3. Torpedo combat command post
4. Type 90 3m range finder
5. Foremast
6. Type 90 triple-torpedo launcher (3)
7. 90cm Searchlight
8. Type 14 2m range finder
9. Mainmast
10. Type 94 depth-charge projector
11. Machinery room
12. Aft boiler room with two Kanpon 285lb/square inch boilers
13. Forward boiler room with two Kanpon 285lb/square inch boilers

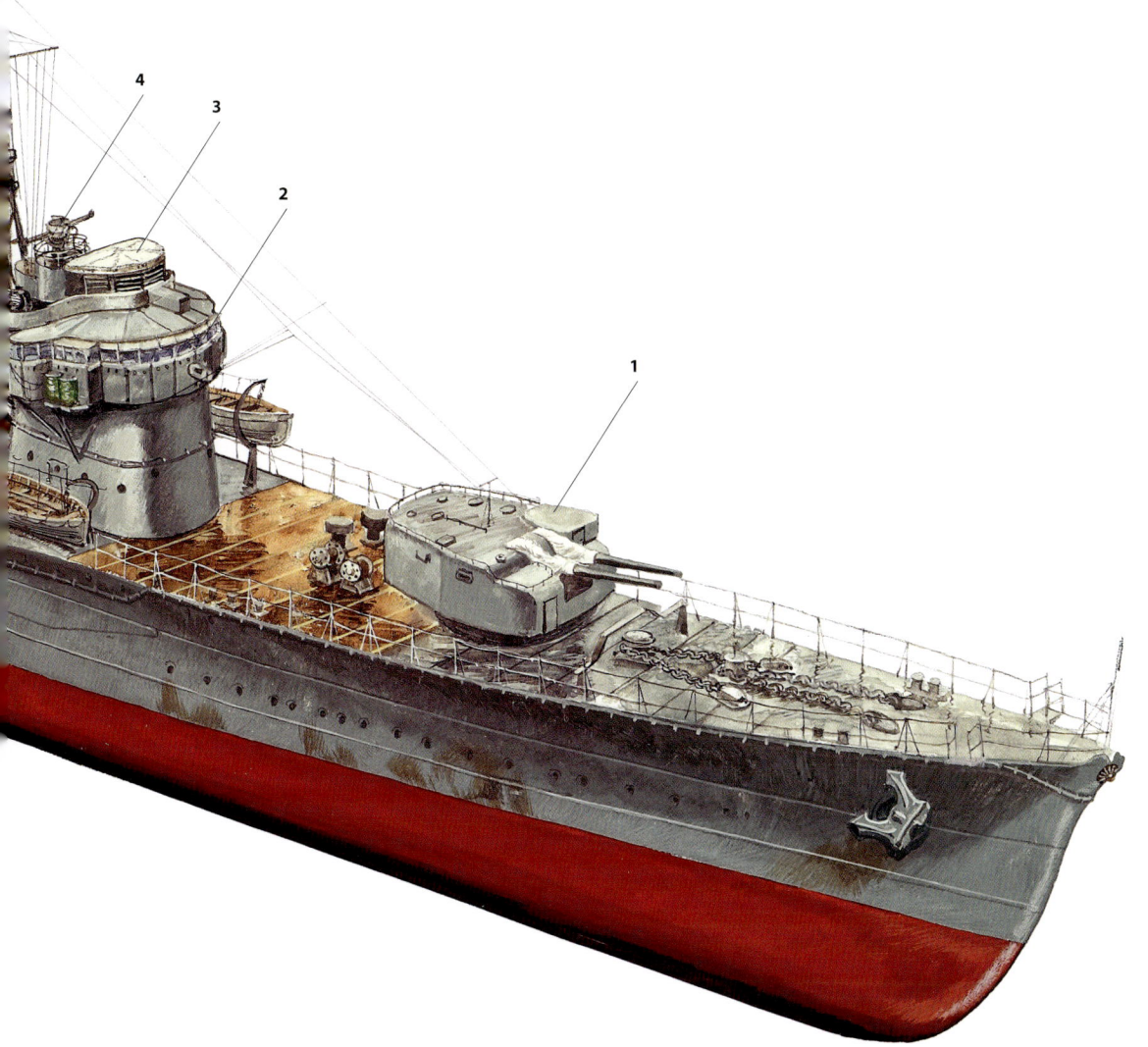

Fubuki Class Specifications (as completed)	
Displacement	Standard: 1,750 tons
Dimensions	Length: 388ft 6in. overall / Beam: 34ft / Draft: 10ft 6in.
Speed	35kt
Range	5,000nm at 14kt
Crew	197

AKATSUKI CLASS

Design and Construction

The last four Special Type destroyers incorporated enough differences that they were given a new class name. The primary difference was that these ships only had three boilers, which meant that the forward stack was thinner than for Group I and II units. This was due to a new, larger type of boiler, which operated at a higher pressure and which produced the same 50,000 SHP with three boilers as earlier ships did with four. The smaller forward funnel became the primary recognition feature for the Akatsuki class (or Group III) compared to earlier units.

Akatsuki Class (Special Type Group III) Construction				
Ship	Built at	Laid down	Launched	Completed
Akatsuki	Sasebo Naval Shipyard	02/17/30	05/07/32	11/30/32
Hibiki	Maizuru Navy Yard	02/15/30	12/22/32	03/30/33
Ikazuchi	Uraga	03/07/30	10/22/31	08/15/32
Inazuma	Fujinagata (Osaka)	03/07/30	02/25/32	11/15/32

In addition to the smaller funnel, the Akatsuki class had a larger bridge structure, because of the addition of another level to provide improved fire control facilities. These four ships incorporated many weight-saving measures, and *Hibiki* was the first all-welded Japanese ship. This meant that displacement was less than earlier Special Type destroyers, but the Akatsuki class still displayed the same stability problems as earlier Special Type units, and had to be rebuilt in the same manner described above.

Group II units *Akebono* and *Ushio* pictured before their reconstruction. Both ships still have their large bridge structures. The ships had long war careers, with *Ushio* being the only Fubuki-class ship to survive the war. (Naval History and Heritage Command)

Group III Special Type unit *Hibiki* seen off the Chinese coast in the late 1930s. The view is taken after the ship had undergone reconstruction, as is seen by the reduced size of the bridge. *Hibiki* survived the war and was handed over to the Soviet Union as reparations. After being rearmed with Russian weapons, she served until 1953 in the Pacific Ocean Fleet. (Naval History and Heritage Command)

Armament and Service Modification

The Group III destroyers were armed like the other Special Type units. They were completed with shields to their torpedo mounts, unlike ships in earlier groups. In 1936, these ships underwent the same reconstruction as the earlier Group I and II units to correct the stability problems. When complete, tonnage was raised to 1,980 tons, which reduced speed to 34kt.

The class began the war with two 13mm twin mounts positioned in front of the second stack. By late 1943, another twin 13mm mount was added in front of the bridge to the three surviving units. This was replaced by a twin 25mm gun on *Hibiki* and *Ikazuchi* by January 1944. These ships had one of their aft 5in. mounts removed and replaced by two triple 25mm mounts by April 1944, and another two triple 25mm mounts were added between the aft torpedo mounts. The last surviving unit, *Hibiki*, had another 20 single 25mm guns added, as well as a No. 22 and 13 radar, before the end of the war.

Wartime Service

Akatsuki: She participated in the invasions of Malaya, the Dutch East Indies, and later the Philippines during the first months of the war. She was assigned to the Kiska invasion force for the Aleutians operation in June 1942. She arrived in the Rabaul area in October 1942 and participated in three transport runs and one sweep mission to Guadalcanal. She was involved in the First Naval Battle of Guadalcanal on November 13, 1942, during which she was sunk by American cruiser and destroyer gunfire.

Ikazuchi operating off the Chinese coast during 1938. Before the war, Japanese destroyers took turns operating off China in wartime conditions, giving their crews valuable combat experience. *Ikazuchi* was sunk by submarine attack in April 1944 with no survivors. (Naval History and Heritage Command)

Hibiki shown on December 10, 1941 conducting operations in the South China as part of the Japanese invasion of Malaya. *Hibiki* was the only Group III unit to survive the war. (Yamato Museum)

Hibiki: She participated in the invasions of Malaya, the Dutch East Indies and later the Philippines during the first months of the war. She was assigned to the Kiska invasion force for the Aleutians operation in June 1942. She was damaged off Kiska by air attack on June 12 and forced to return to Japan. She subsequently performed escort operations in the Central Pacific, and later participated in the evacuation of Kiska in July 1943. In June 1944, she was involved in the Battle of the Philippine Sea. She suffered heavy damage, probably by a mine, on September 6, 1944. She returned to service in January 1945 and was damaged again by a mine in March. She survived the war and was then used as a repatriation ship. In April 1947, she was turned over to the Soviets as reparations and renamed *Pritky*.

Ikazuchi: Her first combat operation was supporting the invasion of Hong Kong in December 1941, during which she participated in the sinking of two British gunboats. She subsequently supported the invasion of the Dutch East Indies in February 1942 and mop-up actions in the Philippines in March. She was assigned to the Northern Force Main Body for the Aleutians operation in June. She arrived at Rabaul in October 1942 and participated in three transport runs and one sweep mission to Guadalcanal. She was part of the First Naval Battle of Guadalcanal on November 13. She claimed to have sunk the American cruiser *Atlanta* with torpedoes; either *Ikazuchi* or *Inazuma* was responsible. She suffered medium damage from gunfire and was forced to return to Japan for repairs. In February 1943, she was assigned to northern waters and participated in the March 26 Battle of the Komandorski Islands. She returned to the Central Pacific to conduct escort duties, and was sunk by the American submarine *Harder* 200 miles south-southeast of Guam on April 14, 1944.

Inazuma: With *Ikazuchi*, her first combat operation was to support the invasion of Hong Kong in December 1941, and she participated in the sinking of two British gunboats. She was damaged by a collision on January 20, 1942. On March 1, she participated in the action that saw the sinking of the British heavy cruiser *Exeter* and an American and a British destroyer. *Inazuma* claimed two torpedo hits on *Exeter*. She was assigned to the Northern Force Main Body for the Aleutians operation in June. She arrived at Truk in October and participated in the First Naval Battle of Guadalcanal. On November 14–15, she was involved in the Second Naval Battle of Guadalcanal and assisted in the sinking of three American destroyers. Later that month, operating out of Rabaul, she conducted several transport missions to points in the Solomons and New Guinea. In February 1943, she was assigned to northern waters and participated in the Battle of the Komandorski Islands. She returned to the Central Pacific to conduct escort duties, and was sunk by the American submarine *Bonefish* near Tawi-Tawi on May 14, 1944.

Akatsuki Class Specifications (as completed)	
Displacement	Standard: 1,680 tons
Dimensions	Length: 389ft overall / Beam: 34ft / Draft: 11ft
Speed	38kt
Range	5,000nm at 14kt
Crew	197

HATSUHARU CLASS

Design and Construction

Whereas the Special Type destroyers were designed and built without any restrictions, the next class was the first designed under the London Naval Treaty. Unlike the Washington Naval Treaty, which put no restrictions on the size or numbers of destroyers, the London Naval Treaty signed in 1930 capped the Imperial Navy's overall destroyer tonnage (105,500 tons) and the maximum tonnage per ship. The largest permissible destroyer was 1,850 tons, but only 16 percent of the overall tonnage figure could be of this size. The remainder could not exceed 1,500 tons. This meant that the continued construction of the Special Type destroyers was no longer an option.

As usual, when faced by treaty restrictions, the Japanese endeavored to place the greatest possible firepower on a design publically compliant with treaty restrictions. For the Hatsuharu class laid down beginning in 1931, the original requirement was to mount the same armament as on the Special Type destroyers on a design lighter by some 260 tons. Twelve of these ships were envisioned, but eventually only six were built.

Hatsuharu Class Construction				
Ship	Built at	Laid down	Launched	Completed
Ariake	Kobe by Kawasaki	01/14/33	09/23/34	03/25/35
Hatsuharu	Sasebo Naval Shipyard	05/14/31	02/27/33	09/30/33
Hatsushimo	Uraga	01/31/33	11/04/33	09/27/34
Nenohi	Uraga	12/15/31	12/22/32	09/30/33
Wakaba	Sasebo Naval Shipyard	12/12/31	03/18/34	10/31/34
Yugure	Maizuru Naval Shipyard	04/09/33	05/06/34	03/30/35

To pull this off, great scrutiny was placed on weight-saving measures. Electric welding was used extensively and less-powerful machinery was fitted. As on the Akatsuki class, only three boilers were fitted, and these could produce only 42,000 SHP. This translated to a top speed of 36.5kt, which was judged to be adequate.

Hatsuharu in October 1933. This view shows the ship in its original configuration, with a massive bridge structure and the single super-firing 5in. mount forward. It is not hard to imagine that this design was top heavy, and in fact a drastic reconstruction was required before the ship was ready for fleet service. (Yamato Museum)

Yugure on October 1935. She was finished to the modified design earlier in the year, and is often referred to as part of the two-ship Ariake class. This beam view shows the modified design created to eliminate the stability problem. The single 5in. gun has been moved to the position abaft the aft deckhouse and the bridge has been significantly reduced in size. The number of torpedo mounts was also reduced from three to two. (Yamato Museum)

The weight-saving efforts were negated by the adoption of a large bridge structure, similar to the Group III Special Type units, and a heavy armament. The first two ships, *Hatsuharu* and *Nenohi*, were completed in September 1933. During trials, it was soon apparent that these ships had stability problems, since they would list badly while turning. A bulge was immediately installed but, in March 1934, when the torpedo boat *Tomodzuru* capsized because of stability problems caused by an excessive armament on a ship of limited tonnage, it became imperative that the Hatsuharu class be redesigned. The first two ships were sent to Kure for extensive modification. This included moving the superimposed single 5in. mount to a position aft on the main deck, followed by a rebuilding of the bridge structure, making it smaller and more compact. The aft torpedo mount on the deckhouse was removed and the length of the deckhouse shortened to make room for the single 5in. mount. To further lower the center of gravity, 84 tons of ballast was added. This increased the displacement to 1,715 tons (2,099 tons full load) and the draft to over 11ft, which reduced speed to 33.5kt.

The second pair of ships was finished to this new design, and the final pair, *Ariake* and *Yugure*, was started to the updated design with further minor modifications (these are often referred to as the Ariake class). The other six units of the class were cancelled.

Armament and Service Modifications

Japanese designers almost matched the armament of the Special Type units on the new class. The main gun battery totaled five 5in. guns arranged in a twin mount forward and a single 5in. superimposed mount. This was the first time the Japanese used this design feature on a destroyer. A second twin 5in. mount was fitted aft. Torpedo armament matched the Fubuki class, with three triple mounts. The difference was that one of the two mounts fitted aft on the Hatsuharu class was placed on top of the aft deckhouse. This was the first class designed to carry the new Type 93 oxygen torpedo. Each of the mounts was provided with reloads. The aft stack was fitted off the centerline because of the placement of the torpedo reloads.

E — THE SPECIAL TYPE DESTROYERS

The top and middle profiles in this plate show *Akebono*, a Group II Special Type, in her 1944 late-war configuration. One of her Type B 5in. gun mounts has been removed and replaced by two triple 25mm mounts. Other additional antiaircraft mounts can be seen forward of the bridge (a twin 25mm), between the aft torpedo mounts (two triple 25mm), and at various locations along the length of the ship (single 25mm guns). Note the No. 22 radar on the foremast and the No. 13 radar on the mainmast. The bottom profile is *Akatsuki*, a Group III Special Type. The ship is in her 1942 configuration, as she appeared just before being sunk in the Second Naval Battle of Guadalcanal in November 1942. Note the thin forward funnel, which was the main distinguishing feature of Group III units.

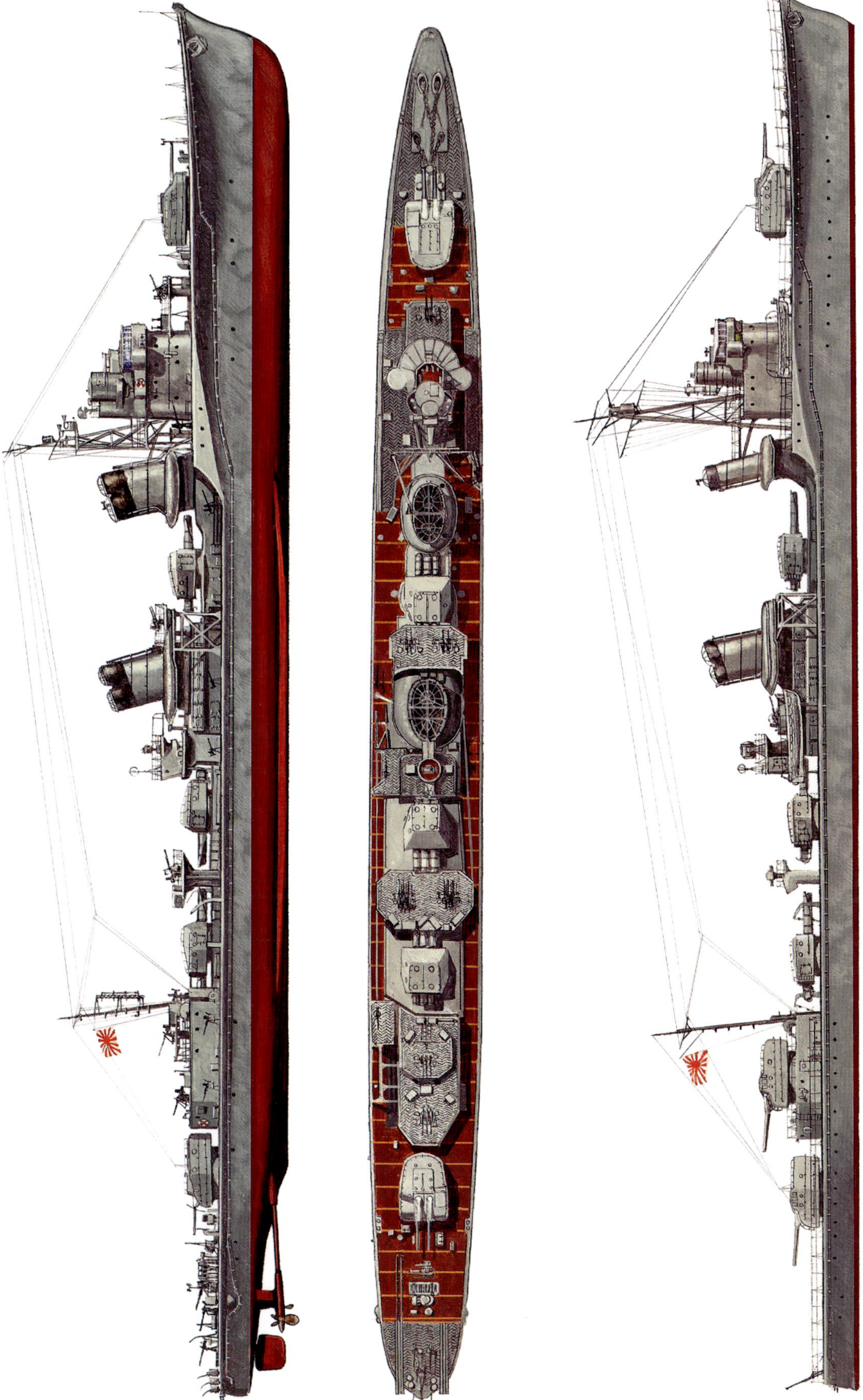

Anti-aircraft armament was limited to two single 40mm guns fitted just forward of the second stack. For anti-submarine work, a single Type 94 projector and a stern depth-charge rack was fitted.

After the extensive modifications already described were completed by 1937, the ships received no further alterations before the start of the war. Modifications during the war revolved around augmentation of the anti-aircraft armament. Beginning in 1942, the ships received a twin 25mm mount in front of the bridge, and the 40mm guns were replaced by twin 25mm mounts. In 1943, the surviving ships had the single 5in. gun mount removed and replaced with a triple 25mm mount. The reload torpedoes for the aft torpedo mounts were also removed. Into 1944, ships began to receive single 25mm guns arranged along the length of the ship and augmented by four 13mm single mounts fitted amidships. The depth-charge load was increased to 36. Half of the class received a No. 22 radar on the foremast and later a No. 13 on the mainmast.

Wartime Service

Ariake: The ship was assigned to Destroyer Division 27 at the start of the war, with her sister ship *Yugure*. In February 1942, she went to escort the Carrier Striking Force during operations supporting the invasion of the Dutch East Indies, and also escorted the Striking Force during the Battle of the Coral Sea in May. She was assigned to the Aleutians Guard Force during the Midway operation. By September 1942, she was active conducting missions in the waters off Guadalcanal, with a total of eight transport missions and one sweep mission being recorded, until she was damaged by air attack in December. She was forced to return to Japan for repairs, but was back at Rabaul by July 1943. She was sunk by B-25 air attack on July 28, 1943, while assisting the grounded destroyer *Mikazuki* near Cape Gloucester.

Hatsuharu: She began the war assigned to Destroyer Division 21 with *Hatsushimo*, *Nenohi*, and *Wakaba*. Her first combat operation was in January 1942 during the invasion of the Dutch East Indies. She participated in the occupation of Attu in the Aleutians in June 1942 and remained in northern waters until October, when she was damaged by B-26 air attack near Kiska. After repairs and modifications, she performed general escort duties, primarily in the Central Pacific, until October 1944, when she was assigned to the 2nd Diversion Attack Force before the Battle of Leyte Gulf. She survived and returned to Manila to be assigned to escort duties for convoys to Ormoc, Leyte. She was sunk by air attack on Manila on November 13, 1944.

Hatsushimo: Her first combat operation was in January 1942, during the invasion of the Dutch East Indies. She participated in the occupation of Attu in the Aleutians in June 1942 and remained in northern waters until August 1943. She was involved in the Battle of the Komandorski Islands in March 1943 and the successful evacuation of the garrison from Kiska in the Aleutians in July 1943. She was present at the Battle of the Philippine Sea in June 1944, and in October 1944 was assigned to the 2nd Diversion Attack Force. She survived and returned to Manila to be assigned escort duties for convoys to Ormoc, Leyte. She returned to Japan in February 1945 and was assigned as escort to the super battleship *Yamato* during her sortie to Okinawa in April. She survived that operation but was sunk by a mine while under American carrier air attack near Maizuru on July 30, 1945. *Hatsushimo* was the last Japanese destroyer sunk in the war.

Nenohi: Her first combat operation was in January 1942 in support of the invasion of the Dutch East Indies. She participated in the occupation of Attu in

June 1942 and remained in northern waters until July 4, 1942, when she was torpedoed by the American submarine *Triton* southeast of Attu.

Wakaba: Her first combat operation was in January 1942 during the invasion of the Dutch East Indies. She participated in the occupation of Attu and remained in northern waters until May 1944. She was involved in the Battle of the Komandorski Islands in March 1943 and the successful evacuation of the garrison from Kiska in July 1943. She was present at the Battle of the Philippine Sea in June 1944, and in October 1944 she was assigned to the 2nd Diversion Attack Force. She was sunk on October 24, 1944 by an American carrier air attack west of Panay.

Yugure: She was assigned to Destroyer Division 27 at the start of the war. In February 1942, she was assigned to escort Carrier Striking Force during operations supporting the invasion of the Dutch East Indies and later escorted the force during the Battle of the Coral Sea in May. She was part of the Aleutians Guard Force during the Midway operation. By September, she was active conducting missions to the waters off Guadalcanal, with a total of six transport missions and one sweep mission in addition to other missions elsewhere in the Solomons. In July 1943, she was active in the Central Solomons and involved in the Battle of Kolombangara, in which Japanese destroyers sank an American destroyer and damaged two light cruisers. On July 20, 1943, she was sunk by aircraft north-northwest of Kolombangara Island, with no survivors.

Hatsuharu Class Specifications (as completed)	
Displacement	Standard: 1,490 tons / Full Load: 1,802 tons
Dimensions	Length: 359ft overall / Beam: 33ft / Draft: 10ft
Speed	36.5kt
Range	6,000nm at 15kt
Crew	228

SHIRATSUYU CLASS

Design and Construction

The stability problems that necessitated the redesign of the Hatsuharu class forced the final six units to be cancelled. After the problem had been rectified, these six ships re-emerged as a new class, named the Shiratsuyu class. The redesign caused the new class to be over the tonnage restrictions set by the London Naval Treaty, but this did not concern the Japanese. Another four ships were authorized in 1934, so the class total reached ten units.

Shiratsuyu Class Construction			
Ship	Built at	Laid down	Launched	Completed
Shiratsuyu	Sasebo Naval Shipyard	11/14/33	04/05/35	08/20/36
Shigure	Uraga	12/09/33	05/18/35	09/07/36
Murasame	Fujinagata (Osaka)	02/01/34	06/20/35	01/07/37
Yudachi	Sasebo Naval Shipyard	10/16/34	06/21/36	01/07/37
Samidare	Uraga	12/19/34	07/06/35	01/29/37
Harusame	Maizuru Naval Shipyard	02/03/35	09/21/35	08/26/37
Yamakaze	Uraga	05/25/35	02/21/36	01/30/37
Kawakaze	Fujinagata (Osaka)	04/25/35	11/01/36	04/30/37
Umikaze	Maizuru Naval Shipyard	05/04/35	11/27/36	05/31/37
Suzukaze	Uraga	07/09/35	03/11/37	08/31/37

Umikaze running trials in April 1937 before being commissioned the next month. The similarity to the preceding Hatsuharu class is obvious. (Yamato Museum)

Overall, the appearance of the Shiratsuyu class resembled that of the preceding Hatsuharu class, particularly with regard to the layout of the armament. The hull was similar to that class, but the forecastle was shorter and the stern longer. The Shiratsuyu class had a greater displacement; to compensate the bridge was redesigned and made more compact and the height of the bridge structure reduced. The same propulsion system from the Hatsuharu class was fitted and, with the greater weight and deeper draft, maximum speed was reduced to 34kt. The asymmetrical arrangement of the stacks on the Hatsuharu class was not repeated.

Armament and Service Modifications

The Shiratsuyu class featured an advancement in the torpedo armament of Japanese destroyers. Two new Type 92 quad mounts were fitted and eight reloads provided for a total of 16 torpedoes. These ships were the first to be fitted with telephone communications to the torpedo stations.

The main gun battery was identical to that on the Hatsuharu-class ships. *Yudachi* had the Type B gun house fitted, but all others were equipped with the Type C 5in. gun house. Originally, the anti-aircraft weapons fit was two single 40mm guns on the first six units and the Type 93 twin 13mm machine gun mount on the last four ships.

The anti-submarine fit on the Shiratsuyu ships was reinforced. Two Type 94 projectors were fitted on the stern, with two stern depth-charge racks. A total of 36 depth charges were carried.

Wartime modifications focused on augmentation of the ships' anti-aircraft fit. The first modification was the addition of a twin 25mm mount forward of the bridge. Beginning in late 1942, the single aft 5in. gun mount was removed and replaced by a triple 25mm mount. With two triple mounts amidships, the normal light anti-aircraft gun configuration going into 1943 was three triple and one twin 25mm mounts.

In 1944, the anti-aircraft fit of surviving ships was reinforced further. At least *Samidare*, *Shigure*, and *Umikaze* received an additional ten single mounts located along the length of the ship. In December 1944, *Shigure* received another five single

F **HATSUHARU AND SHIRATSUYU CLASSES**
Hatsushimo (Hatsuharu class) as she appeared in April 1945, accompanying super battleship *Yamato* on her final sortie. This plate, in profile and overhead, shows the ship in her late-war configuration. Note the removal of the single 5in. mount aft and its replacement with a triple 25mm mount. Two additional triple 25mm mounts are positioned between the Type 90 triple-torpedo launchers, and a twin 25mm mount is located forward of the bridge. A No. 22 radar has been fitted on the foremast and a No. 13 radar on the mainmast. The second ship is *Yudachi* (Shiratsuyu class) as she appeared in 1942 before she was sunk in the Second Naval Battle of Guadalcanal in November that year. Her overall appearance is similar to the Hatsuharu class, but with the Type C 5in. mounts and a smaller bridge structure. The single 5in. mount is still retained aft. The two torpedo launchers are Type 92 quad mounts.

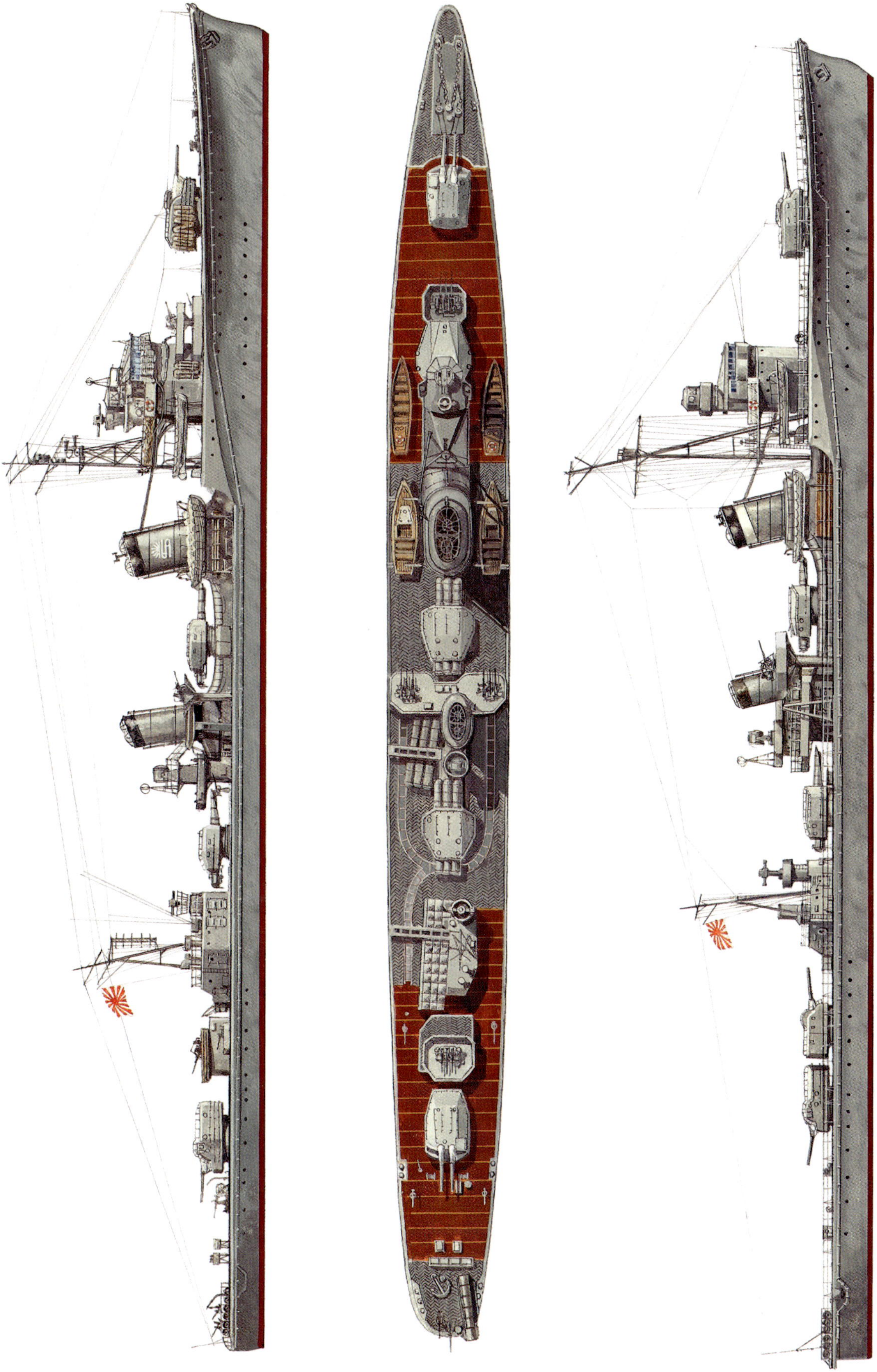

Yamakze on trials in May 1937 before being commissioned in July. The Shiratsuyu class featured a compact bridge design and was the first Japanese destroyer to carry the Type 92 quadruple torpedo mounts, two of which can be seen in this view. (Yamato Museum)

LEFT
Yamakaze sinking, as seen through the periscope of submarine *Nautilus*. The ship was torpedoed off the Japanese coast on June 25, 1942. Her entire crew of 227 was killed in the attack. (Naval History and Heritage Command)

RIGHT
This dramatic photo is of *Harusame* seen through the periscope of American submarine *Wahoo* near Wewak, New Guinea on January 24, 1943. The ship was heavily damaged, but returned to Japan for repairs only to be lost the following year to air attack. (Naval History and Heritage Command)

25mm mounts and four single 13mm machine guns. By 1944, the surviving ships had their spare torpedoes removed to reduce top weight. Ships still in service by 1944 also received radar, with both a No. 22 and a No. 13 set being fitted on the foremast.

Wartime Service

Harusame: She began the war as part of Destroyer Division 4 and was assigned to support the invasion of the Philippines and later the Dutch East Indies. She participated in the Battle of the Java Sea on February 27, 1942. She was assigned to the invasion force for the Midway operation. In August, she was dispatched to the South Pacific, where she participated in the Battle of the Eastern Solomons. She conducted seven transport missions to Guadalcanal. On November 13, she participated in the First Naval Battle of Guadalcanal, but was not heavily engaged. On January 24, 1943, at Wewak, New Guinea, she was torpedoed and heavily damaged by the American submarine *Wahoo*. She returned to service in November 1943 and, in February 1944, was damaged by a carrier air attack on Truk. On June 8, while on a transport run to Biak Island off northern New Guinea, she was bombed and sunk by American B-25s.

Kawakaze: She was assigned to Destroyer Division 24 at the start of the war and participated in the invasions of the Philippines and the Dutch East Indies. In February 1942, she participated in the Battle of the Java Sea and the sinking of the British heavy cruiser *Exeter* and an American and British destroyer on March 1, 1942. She was part of the Aleutians Guard Force during the Midway operation in June. In August 1942, she moved to the South Pacific. On the night of August 22, she engaged two American destroyers off Guadalcanal and torpedoed one, which was later scuttled. She participated in the Battle of the Eastern Solomons in late August 1942. She conducted several transport and sweep missions to Guadalcanal, including as escort for the October 13–14 battleship bombardment of Henderson Field. She participated in the Battle of the Santa Cruz Islands in late October. In mid-November, she escorted a troop convoy to Guadalcanal. On November 30, she participated in the Battle of Tassafaronga, in which Japanese torpedoes sank one American heavy cruiser and damaged three more. She continued to make supply runs to the island and participated in the evacuation of the Japanese garrison in February 1943. She was sunk by American destroyer torpedoes and gunfire at the Battle of Vella Gulf on August 6, 1943.

Murasame: She began the war assigned to Destroyer Division 4 and supported the invasion of the Philippines and later the Dutch East Indies. She participated in the Battle of the Java Sea. She was assigned to the invasion force for the Midway operation. In August 1942, she was dispatched to the South Pacific. She conducted seven transport missions to Guadalcanal. On November 13, she was part of the First Naval Battle of Guadalcanal. In the van of the Japanese force, *Murasame* was heavily engaged; she torpedoed the American light cruiser *Juneau* and later probably finished off an American destroyer, also using torpedoes. She emerged with only minor damage. She was sunk on a transport run to Kolombangara in the Central Solomons on March 6, 1943, after being disabled by gunfire and then struck by a torpedo.

Samidare: She was assigned to Destroyer Division 2 and saw service like the other ships in this squadron in the initial phase of the war. In August 1942, she was committed to the Solomons campaign and participated in the Battle of the Eastern Solomons. She was involved in the First Naval Battle of Guadalcanal on November 13, and returned two nights later to take part in the Second Naval Battle of Guadalcanal, where she assisted in the sinking of three American destroyers and the damaging of a fourth. In February 1943, she covered the evacuation of Guadalcanal, and in April she conducted several transport runs to other points in the Solomons. In July–August 1943, she shifted to the Northern Pacific to take part in the evacuation of Kiska. She participated in the Battle of Vella Lavella on October 6, 1943, where either she or *Shigure* torpedoed an American destroyer. In November, she participated in the Battle of Empress Augusta Bay and was damaged in a collision with *Shiratsuyu*. She was probably responsible for torpedoing and damaging an American destroyer. In June 1944, she participated in the unsuccessful Biak operation and later in the month was involved in the Battle of the Philippine Sea. She was sunk on August 25 near Palau by the American submarine *Batfish*.

Shiratsuyu: She was assigned to Destroyer Division 27 at the start of the war, and remained in home waters until May 1942, when she was assigned to escort the Carrier Striking Force at the Battle of the Coral Sea. During the Midway operation, she was part of the Aleutians Guard Force. She moved to the South Pacific and escorted a mid-October convoy to Guadalcanal; after this she conducted another four transport runs and one sweep mission to Guadalcanal. In November 1942, she was damaged by a B-17 attack and forced to return to Japan. She came back to the Solomons and participated in the Battle of Empress Augusta Bay in November 1943, where she was damaged in a collision with the destroyer *Samidare*. She was involved in the unsuccessful Biak operation in June 1944 and was damaged by air attack. On June 15, 1944, she was sunk in a collision with the tanker *Seiyo Maru* southeast of Surigao Strait.

Shigure: The most famous ship of the Shiratsuyu class, she became known as the Indestructible Destroyer as a result of her service in the Solomons, during which she sustained no casualties during heavy operations. Her early war service was similar to the other ships of Destroyer Division 27. By October 1942, she was operating out of Rabaul and conducted nine transport missions to Guadalcanal, including escort of the mid-October convoy. She returned to Rabaul in July 1943 and began a period of constant operations, which included the Battle of Vella Gulf in August, when she was the only Japanese destroyer to survive, the Battle off Horaniu, in which she again engaged American destroyers, the Battle of Vella Lavella in October, in which her torpedoes contributed to the sinking of an American destroyer, and the Battle of Empress Augusta Bay in November. She was damaged by an American carrier air attack on February 17, 1944, at Truk.

She participated in the unsuccessful Biak operation in June 1944, during which she was damaged by an Allied cruiser-destroyer task force. She was involved in the Battle of the Philippine Sea in June 1944, and at the Battle of Leyte Gulf. She saw action at the Battle of Surigao Strait and was the only ship to survive from the Japanese Southern Force. On January 24, 1945, she was torpedoed and sunk by the American submarine *Blackfin*, east of Malaya.

Suzukaze: She was assigned to Destroyer Division 24 at the start of the war and participated in the invasions of the Philippines and the Dutch East Indies. On February 4, 1942, she was torpedoed by the American submarine *Sculpin* and heavily damaged. She returned to service in July and was sent to the South Pacific, where she participated in the Battle of the Eastern Solomons in August. From August 1942 until February 1943, she took part in over ten transport runs to Guadalcanal and five combat missions to the island, including participation in the Battle of Tassafaronga in November 1942. She was also involved in the carrier Battle of the Santa Cruz Islands in October 1942. She covered the evacuation of Guadalcanal in February 1943, and then participated in the Battle of Kula Gulf in July, where she was damaged by American cruiser gunfire. She was sunk on January 26, 1944 by the American submarine *Skipjack* near Ponape Island.

Umikaze: She began the war assigned to Destroyer Division 24 and participated in the invasion of the Philippines and the Dutch East Indies. She was present at the Battle of the Java Sea in February 1942, but saw no action. She was assigned to the Aleutians Guard Force as part of the Midway operation. She was moved to the South Pacific in August 1942, where she conducted ten transport missions to Guadalcanal and three combat missions. She participated in the Battle of the Santa Cruz Islands in October, and on November 18 incurred heavy bomb damage from a B-17 attack. She was back in service in February 1943 and returned to Rabaul to conduct transport missions to various points in the Solomons. While on escort duties in the Central Pacific, she was torpedoed and sunk by the American submarine *Guardfish* on February 1, 1944, near Truk.

Yamakaze: She began the war assigned to Destroyer Division 24 and participated in the invasion of the Philippines and the Dutch East Indies. On February 11, 1942, she attacked and sank the American submarine *Shark* with 5in. gunfire east of Manado. She participated in the Battle of the Java Sea and the March 1, 1942 action against American and British ships. She was assigned to the Aleutians Guard Force as part of the Midway operation. On June 25, 1942, she was sunk by the American submarine *Nautilus* near Yokosuka, with no survivors.

Yudachi: She was assigned to Destroyer Division 4 and conducted operations as other ships in this unit during the initial period of the war. By August 1942, she was committed to operations in the Solomons. She participated in 13 transport missions and five sweep missions to Guadalcanal. On a mission on September 5, 1942, she played the primary role in the sinking of two American destroyer transports. On November 13, 1942, she engaged in the First Naval Battle of Guadalcanal. In the van of the Japanese force with *Murasame*, she torpedoed the

G   **SHIGURE AT THE BATTLE OF SURIGAO STRAIT, OCTOBER 25, 1944**
Shigure was known as a lucky ship, and her luck continued to hold on this occasion. Despite damage from a shell hit and many near misses, she was the only ship from the 2nd Diversionary Attack Force to survive the battle. In a sign that the Japanese destroyers had lost their fighting edge, she left the battle not having fired any of her torpedoes. The late-war modification to Shiratsuyu-class ships can be seen in this view, with the aft single 5in. gun being removed and replaced by a triple 25mm mount.

American heavy cruiser *Portland*, but was heavily damaged by American cruiser and destroyer gunfire, abandoned, and later sank.

Shiratsuyu Class Specifications (as completed)	
Displacement	Standard: 1,685 tons / Full Load: 1,980 tons
Dimensions	Length: 353ft overall / Beam: 32ft 6in. / Draft: 11ft 6in.
Speed	34kt
Range	6,000nm at 15kt
Crew	180

ANALYSIS AND CONCLUSION

The Imperial Navy's destroyer force went to war possessing some of the most powerful ships in the world. However, an assessment of its strengths and weaknesses reveals that these ships were suited for only a single mission: delivering torpedo attacks. Overall, Japanese destroyers were excellent torpedo boats, but were not well-balanced destroyers, since they were deficient in anti-aircraft and anti-submarine warfare capabilities. In the early part of the war, with patchy Allied resistance and during the series of night battles in the Solomons against American surface ships, Japanese destroyers were well suited for the roles they were tasked to execute, and as a result performed excellently. However, as the war went on and the Americans brought increasing numbers of submarines into play and gained air superiority over the battle areas, the weaknesses of Japanese destroyers were ruthlessly exposed. The table below provides the causes of loss for the 74 Japanese destroyers covered in this book.

Japanese Destroyer Losses 1941–45 by Cause					
Class (Number)	Surface	Submarine	Air	Other	Surviving
Minekaze (13)	0	7	1	0	5
Kamikaze (9)	0	4	2	1	2
Mutsuki (12)	1	1	10	0	0
Fubuki (19)	3	6	7	2	1
Akatsuki (4)	1	2	0	0	1
Hatsuharu (6)	0	1	4	1	0
Shiratsuyu (10)	3	5	1	1	0
Totals	8	26	25	5	9

By far the leading causes of loss were submarine and air attack. Losses in surface actions were relatively minor. Other causes of losses included mining, collisions, and a single loss to shore batteries. It is notable that only two destroyers used as front-line units survived the war. Losses increased throughout the war, with only four being lost in 1941, 12 in 1942, 14 in 1943, an astounding 30 in 1944, and four in 1945.

A review of each class supports this basic assessment of the strengths and weaknesses of the Japanese destroyer force. At the start of the war, the Minekaze class was considered obsolescent by the Japanese. Most were assigned to secondary commands and undertook general patrol and escort duties. In this capacity, the Minekaze class proved to be undistinguished submarine hunters, since its ships lacked modern sensors or anti-submarine weapons. Of the 13 ships, only five survived, and of the eight lost, seven were sunk by submarines.

The Kamikaze class formed two destroyer divisions at the beginning of the war and was briefly active in the forward areas before being assigned escort duties in rear areas. Of the nine ships, seven were lost, with submarines again being the primary agent of destruction.

The 12-ship Mutsuki class saw extensive service during the war, and all 12 were lost before the end of 1944. Unlike the previous two classes of older destroyers, they were employed in the forward areas, with almost the entire class seeing duty in the Solomons campaign. Ten units were lost to air attack, clearly demonstrating the inability of these ships to deal with concerted air assault. One ship was lost in surface action and, unusually, only a single ship was sunk by submarine attack.

After addressing their stability faults, the 19 Group I and II Special Type destroyers rendered good service. Fubuki-class units saw extensive action in the Solomons area, but were eventually assigned secondary duties as newer destroyers entered the fleet. Only one ship, *Ushio*, survived the war. Of the 18 ships sunk, six were lost to submarine attack, seven to air attack, three to surface action, and two were mined. Of the four Group III Special Type ships, only one survived.

The original Hatsuharu design also possessed severe stability problems that were corrected before the war. None of the six units survived, and four of these were sunk by air attack. The similar Shiratsuyu class also saw extensive service, with none of the ten ships surviving the war. Only one ship was sunk by air, but five were destroyed by submarine attack and three sunk in surface engagements.

BIBLIOGRAPHY

Campbell, John, *Naval Weapons of World War Two*, Conway Maritime Press (2002)
Dull, Paul, *A Battle History of the Imperial Japanese Navy (1941–1945)*, Naval Institute Press (1978)
Evans, David C., and Peattie, Mark R., *Kaigun*, Naval Institute Press (1997)
Friedman, Norman, *Naval Radar*, Conway Maritime Press (1981)
Fukui, Shizuo, *Japanese Naval Vessels at the End of World War II*, Naval Institute Press (1991)
Itani, Jiro, Lengerer, Hans, and Rehm-Takahara, Tomoko, "Japanese Oxygen Torpedoes and Fire Control Systems," *Warship 1991*, Conway Maritime Press (1991)
Jentscura, Hansgeorg, Jung, Dieter, and Mickel, Peter, *Warships of the Imperial Japanese Navy, 1869-1945*, Naval Institute Press (1977)
Mutsuki Class Destroyers, Gakken Publishing (2008)
O'Hara, Vincent P., *The US Navy Against the Axis*, Naval Institute Press (2007)
Preston, Anthony (ed.), *Super Destroyers*, Conway Maritime Press (1978)
Special Type Destroyers, Gakken Publishing (2010)
"Genealogy of Japanese Destroyers Part 1," *Warship Model Magazine*, 17, Model Art Co. (2005)
"Genealogy of Japanese Destroyers Part 2," *Warship Model Magazine*, 25, Model Art Co. (2007)
Warship Mechanism Picturebook Japanese Destroyers, Grand Prix Publishing (1995)
Watts, A. J. and Gordon, B. G., *The Imperial Japanese Navy*, MacDonald & Company (1971)
Whitley, M. J., *Destroyers of World War Two*, Naval Institute Press (1988)
www.combinedfleet.com/lancers.htm

INDEX

Numbers in **bold** refer to plates and illustrations

Akatsuki 32, 33, **E** (36)
Akatsuki class 32–35, 46
Akebono 22, 25, **27**, **32**, **E** (36)
Akikaze 8, 10
Albacore, USS 27
Aleutians operation (1942) 11, 25, 26, 28, 29, 33, 34, 38, 39, 42, 43, 44
Amagiri 22, 25–26
Andaman Islands 25–26, 27, 28, 29
Ariake 35, 36, 38
armament and service modifications 4, 6, 6–8
    Akatsuki class 33
    Fubuki class 24–25
    Hatsuharu class 36–38
    Kamikaze class 14
    Minekaze class 9, 9–10, **12**, **A** (12)
    Mutsuki class 17
    Shiratsuyu class 40–42
Asagiri 22, 26
Asakaze 14
Asanagi 14
Atlanta, USS 34
Ayanami 22, 26, **29**

Biak operation (1944) 43, 44
Bismarck Sea, Battle of the (1943) 28
Blackfin, USS 44
Bonefish, USS 34
British Borneo 26, 27, 28

Cape Esperance, Battle of (1942) 26, **D** (30)
Cape St George, Battle of (1943) 20, 26, 29
Chicago, USS **B** (18)
Coral Sea, Battle of the (1942) 14, 15, 18, 20, 25, 28, 38, 39, 43

design and construction
    Akatsuki class 32
    Fubuki class 21–24
    Hatsuharu class 35–36
    Kamikaze class 12–14
    Minekaze class 8–9
    Mutsuki class 16–17
    Shiratsuyu class 39–40
Dutch East Indies 10, 11, 14, 18, 20, 25, 26, 27, 28, 33, 34, 38, 39, 42, 43, 44

Eastern Solomons, Battle of the (1942) 20, 42, 43, 44
Empress Augusta Bay, Battle of (1943) 43
Exeter, HMS 25, 34, 42

Fubuki 22, 24, 26, **C** (22)
Fubuki class 4, 6, **6**, 7, 21–32, **28**, 46, 47, **C** (22)
Fumizuki 16, 17, **21**

Gilbert Islands 14, 15
Grayback, USS 11, 29
Growler, USS 28
Guadalcanal 15, 18, 20, 26, 27, 28, 29, 33, 34, 38, 39, 42, 43, 44, **E** (36), **F** (40)
Guam 20, 21, 27
Guardfish, USS 10, 44

Haddo, USS 14
Hakaze 8, 10
Harder, USS 18, 34
Harukaze 14–15
Harusame 39, 42, **42**
Hatakaze 14, 15
Hatsuharu 35, **35**, 36, 38

Hatsuharu class 6, 35–39, 46, 47, **F** (40)
Hatsushimo 35, 38, **F** (40)
Hatsuyuki 22, 26, **D** (30)
Hayate 14, 15
Hibiki 32, 33, **33**, 34, **34**
Hokaze 8, 11
Hong Kong, invasion of (1941) 34
Houston, USS 14, 27

Ikazuchi 32, 33, **33**, 34
Inazuma 32, 34
Isonami 22, 26

Jarvis, USS **B** (18)
Java Sea, Battle of the (1942) 27, 28, 42, 43, 44

Kamikaze 14, 15, **15**
Kamikaze class **4**, 6, 12–16, 46, 47, **B** (18)
Kavieng 20, 21, **21**
Kawakaze 39, 42
Kikuzuki 16, 17–18
Kisaragi 16, 18
Kiska, invasion of (1942) 11, 33, 34
Kolombangara, Battle of (1943) 18, 20, 39
Komandorski Islands, Battle of the (1943) 29, 34, 38, 39
Kula Gulf, Battle of (1943) 18, 20, **25**, 26, 44

Lae/Salamua invasion force 15, 17, 18, 20, 21
Leyte Gulf, Battle of (1944) 10, 21, 25, 28, 29, 38, 44
London Naval Treaty (1930) 35, 39

Malaya 10, 14, 20, 25–26, 27, 28, 33, 34, **34**
Matsukaze 14, 15
Midway, Battle of (1942) 12, 18, 26
Mikazuki 16, 17, 18, 38
Mikuki 22
Minazuki 16, 18, **20**
Minekaze 8, **9**, 11, **A** (12)
Minekaze class 4, 6, 8–12, **9**, **12**, 46, **A** (12)
Mochizuki 16, 18
Murakumo 22, 27
Murasame 39, 43
Mutsuki 16, 18–20
Mutsuki class **5**, 6, **6**, 16–21, 46, 47, **C** (22)

Nadakaze 10
Nagatsuki 16, 20, **25**
Namikaze 8, 9, 10, 11, **A** (12)
Nautilus, USS 44
Nenohi 35, 36, 38–39
New Guinea 10, 26, 28, 34, 42
Nokaze 8, **9**, 11
Numakaze 8, 9, 11

Oboro 22, 27
Oite 14, 15
Okikaze 8, 11

Paddle, USS 11
Pargo, USS 11
Perch, USS 28
Perth, HMAS 14
Philippine Sea, Battle of the (1944) 16, 20, 34, 38, 39, 43, 44
Picuda, USS 16
Pintado, USS 10
Pogy, USS 11
Pollack, USS 14
Portland, USS 46

radar 7–8

Sagiri 22, 27
Sailfish, USS 15
Samidare 39, 40, 43
Santa Cruz Islands, Battle of the (1942) 42, 44
Satsuki 16, 17, 20
Savo Island, Battle of (1942) 16, **B** (18)
Sawakaze 8, 10, 11
Sazanami 22, 27
Sculpin, USS 44
Shark, USS 44
Shigure 39, 40–42, 43–44, **G** (44)
Shikinami 22, 27–28
Shimakaze 10
Shinonome 22, 28, **29**
Shiokaze 8, 10
Shirakumo 22, 28
Shiratsuyu 39, 43
Shiratsuyu class 7, 39–46, 47, **F** (40)
Shirayuki 22, **27**, 28
Skate, USS 29
Skipjack, USS 44
"Special Type" destroyers *see* Fubuki class
Strong, USS 20
Sumatra 25–26, 27, 28, 29
Sunda Strait, Battle of (1942) 14, 26, 27, 28
Surigao Strait, Battle of (1944) 25, 29, 44, **G** (44)
Suzukaze 39, 44
Swordfish, USS 15

Tachikaze 8, 11–12, **12**
Tassafaronga, Battle of (1942) 42, 44
Tautog, USS 26, 28
Thanet, HMS 26, 29
Thresher, USS 11
Trigger, USS 11
Triton, USS 39
Tulagi invasion force 18, 21

Umikaze 39, 40, **40**, 44
Uranami 22, **27**, 28
Ushio 22, 28–29, **32**, 47
Usugumo 22, 29
Uzuki 16, 17, 20

Vella Gulf, Battle of (1943) 42, 43
Vella Lavella, Battle of (1943) 43

Wahoo, USS 42
Wakaba 35, 39
Wake Island 14, 15, 18
wartime service
    Akatsuki class 33–35
    Fubuki class 25–32
    Hatsuharu class 38–39
    Kamikaze class 14–16
    Minekaze class 10–12
    Mutsuki class 17–21
    Shiratsuyu class 42–46
Washington, USS 26
Washington Navy Treaty (1922) 4, 16, 21

Yakaze 8, 10, 12
Yamakaze 39, **42**, 44
Yayoi 16, 17, 20
Yudachi 39, 40, 44–46, **F** (40)
Yugiri 22, 25, 29
Yugure 35, 36, **36**, 39
Yukaze 8, 10, 12, **A** (12)
Yunagi 14, 15–16, **16**, **B** (18)
Yuzuki 16, 17, 21